A VILLAGE WITHIN A CITY
The Story of Old Headington · Oxford

Edited by
Jean Cook and Leslie Taylor

Published by
THE FRIENDS OF OLD HEADINGTON
OXFORD

First Published 1987 by
© The Friends of Old Headington, Oxford

All rights reserved. No part of this publication may be reproduced, in any form or by any means, without the prior permission of the publisher.

British Library Cataloguing in Publication Data

A village within a city : the story of Old Headington, Oxford.
1. Old Headington (Oxford, Oxfordshire) History
I. Cook, Jean II. Taylor, Leslie
942.5′74   DA690.098

ISBN 0 9506065 1 0

Set in Palatino 10 on 11 point
Designed by Christopher Belson

Acknowledgements

A number of people have contributed to the production of this book and we would like to take this opportunity to thank them. Authors' names are given in the text but there are others who have helped in various ways. They are:

Jane Belson, Grace Briggs, Malcolm Graham, Peter Gray, Elizabeth Leyland, Angelika Ploptsl-Blombach and Penny Richards.

We felt that illustrations would play a very important part and so we have tried not only to find ones which relate closely to the text but also, wherever possible, to choose ones which have not been used before.

We have been fortunate in being able to draw on Mr Alan Edney's collection and on the Friends' albums. Roger France and Max Beresford provided the illustrations for Roger France's section. Christopher Belson has prepared many of the line drawings and has also provided some of the photographs, as has Leslie Taylor. Edith Gollnast has prepared the drawings in John Ashdown's section.

In addition we are grateful to the following institutions for the provision of illustrations and for permission to reproduce material in their possession:

The Bodleian Library, Oxfordshire County Libraries and the Public Record Office.

JMC and LWT

A VILLAGE WITHIN A CITY
The Story of Old Headington · Oxford

Edited by Jean Cook and Leslie Taylor
Designed by Christopher Belson

Introduction and Foreword	4
The geological and geographical setting James Bond	5
The past history of the village Jean Cook and Mary Hodges	11
The parish church Julian Munby	25
Buildings in the village John Ashdown	31
Development and the protection of character Roger France	47
The present century Leslie Taylor	55
Bibliography	64

Introduction

I am glad to welcome another publication from the Friends of Old Headington. In 1977 when I wrote the Foreword to *Within Living Memory: Recollections of Old Headington, Oxford* which Leslie and Griselda Taylor had compiled for the Friends, little did I expect that in the course of a few years a second book would appear.

This new volume, a symposium of six chapters, has been produced because many local people were interested to know more about the history of Old Headington, which was designated a Conservation Area in 1971.

The various authors, all experts in their fields, are an impressive team and have contributed information of a high academic standard in a most readable form.

From the onset, the University Department for External Studies has given valuable support and encouragement to the project and has not only suggested the authors but also introduced the General Editor, Jean Cook - a historian and archaeologist, the first Director of the Oxford City and County Museum at Woodstock and now a free-lance lecturer and editor. She has worked tirelessly for the project and her contribution, in many and various ways, has been invaluable. She has been ably supported by two members of the Friends, both professionals in their own fields: Leslie Taylor, a former educational publisher, and Christopher Belson, a Design Consultant. Their expertise, combined with a personal knowledge of the neighbourhood, has also contributed very greatly to the production and to the attractive appearance of the book. We are greatly indebted to them and to the other contributors - all of whom have most generously given their services.

We are also very grateful to the Trustees of the Pantin Charitable Trust and to the Trustees of the Greening Lamborn Trust for their financial backing which has enabled the Friends' Committee to proceed with the book's production.

At the present time a village Conservation Area, situated within a City boundary, must constantly be under threat especially from increasing traffic and inappropriate development. As the story in the book unfolds, it is clear to see why there is much concern to protect the character of the area. The Friends have done a service by providing expert information as well as the historical perspectives against which present-day policies and problems can be set.

I wish the book every success.

President, The Friends of Old Headington   *Headington House, Old Headington, July 1987*

Foreword

Old Headington is a very special part of Oxford, a suburb which has somehow retained the character of a village. Leslie Taylor describes it as being 'pleasantly hidden away in an oasis on the outskirts of Oxford' and this remarkable blend of remoteness and accessibility has been a crucial element in its development and happy survival.

Proximity to the city has long encouraged the wealthy and not so wealthy to settle in Old Headington and their efforts to beautify the place have created a legacy which this book encourages us to share and enjoy. In modern times, a location away from major routes has helped to protect Old Headington from the rising tide of traffic and commercial development.

A Village within a City could very usefully serve as a model for studies of other communities and begins by placing Old Headington in its geological and geographical context before considering its history. The historical section provides a neat distillation of published sources and although it makes no claim to original research, it does include data from the census enumerators' returns for 1851 and 1881. The results present a picture of increasing prosperity and contrast the virtually static population of Old Headington with the steady growth which was being experienced elsewhere in the parish. John Ashdown remarks upon 'the encirclement of the village by mansions in parks', and this process made Old Headington something of a closed village, influenced and to some extent dominated by the inhabitants of its larger houses. The relationship between gentry and workaday villagers is touched on here, but would clearly merit further study and, dare one say it, another publication by the Friends of Old Headington!

The contextual chapters are followed by John Ashdown's examination of the historic buildings in Old Headington which is more detailed than anything hitherto published and is liberally illustrated with plans and photographs. Roger France looks at past, present and future conservation issues and will probably surprise most people by revealing the scale of recent residential development in this seemingly unchanged and unchanging suburb. The book ends appropriately with Leslie Taylor's personal account of the Old Headington that he has known and loved for over 40 years. He chronicles regrettable changes such as the loss of local shops and growing traffic problems but he also demonstrates that individuals acting alone or in concert can still play a crucial role in the community.

The many people who read and enjoy this book may well be encouraged to find out more for themselves. The bibliography lists major published sources, some of which are obtainable from booksellers or may be borrowed from local branch libraries. All these works and others may be consulted in the County Libraries' Local Studies Collection at Oxford Central Library, which is also a treasure-house of printed maps, photographs, newspapers, census returns and many other Oxford and Oxfordshire resources. From there, the trail may lead on to the County Record Office, the County Museum, the Bodleian Library or to other archive repositories. As this fascinating book makes clear there are many approaches to a local study and the bungalow dweller has every chance of making as valid a contribution as the occupant of the proverbial ivory tower.

Malcolm Graham, August 1987

The geological and geographical setting
James Bond

Introduction

Headington is situated some 2 miles (3km) east of Oxford. The ancient parish of Headington occupied some 2,171 acres (878·5 hectares) prior to the series of administrative alterations which began in 1881, extending from Wick Copse in the north to Bullingdon Green on the south, and from Sandhill on the east to the Marston Road on the west.

The parish straddles the escarpment of the Oxford Heights, a ridge of hills stretching from Faringdon in the west to Brill in the east. These hills are formed by the harder and more permeable Corallian limestones and sandstones, which have been more resistant to erosion than the clays which form the vales to the north and south. The rocks have been gently tilted by earth movements since they were laid down during the Jurassic period, some 150 - 180 million years ago, so that they dip towards the south. This typically creates a steep scarp face to the north and a gentler dip-slope to the south, characteristics clearly seen in the western part of the escarpment towards Faringdon. Around Oxford, however, the folding of the rocks is more complex, although their general dip is still towards the south or south-east, and the hills are higher and rather more broken in character.

Oxford itself is situated at the confluence of the River Thames and the River Cherwell, at the point where the two rivers break through the escarpment. Headington is drained on the north by the Bayswater Brook, a small stream which rises on the eastern slopes of Shotover Hill and then flows westwards to join the Cherwell near New Marston. The valleys of the Bayswater Brook and the Cherwell, which generally form the boundaries of the parish on the north and west, are flat-bottomed and marshy, less than 200 feet (60m) above sea-level. The valley floors are based on Oxford Clay, the oldest stratum to outcrop in this immediate area. The land then rises fairly sharply up to the top of the plateau which is formed by the Calcareous Grit series of the Corallian beds. This plateau generally levels off at around 290-300 feet (c. 90m) above sea-level, though locally it rises to 350 feet (106m) in the vicinity of the Manor House. Headington Hill itself and the slopes north of St Andrew's Church are part of the Calcareous Grit scarp. East of the Nuffield Orthopaedic Centre hospital and Bury Knowle Park the Calcareous Grit is succeeded by the Coral Rag series of the Corallian, and this in turn is capped by Kimeridge Clay to the east of Wood Farm, though these geological changes are not marked by any major changes in relief. The southern flank of this plateau is dissected by the heads of the Moor Ditch and Lye Valley, which meet below the Churchill Hospital, the resulting stream then draining Cowley Marsh and joining the Thames near Iffley. Immediately beyond the eastern boundary of Headington the land rises sharply once again to the summit of Shotover Hill, 562 feet (171m) above sea-level, formed by an isolated flat capping of the later Portland and Wealden Beds.

The River System

Many parts of the Thames river system show evidence of superimposed drainage, whereby a network of rivers and streams which evolved on a blanket of higher strata has completely eroded these, cutting downwards all the time, with the result that it now bears little relationship to the present outcrops. There is evidence of this process even with small streams like the Bayswater Brook and its tributary coming down from Lodge Farm near Stowood, which have cut miniature gorges through the barrier of Corallian beds upfaulted across their path. Important changes to the local

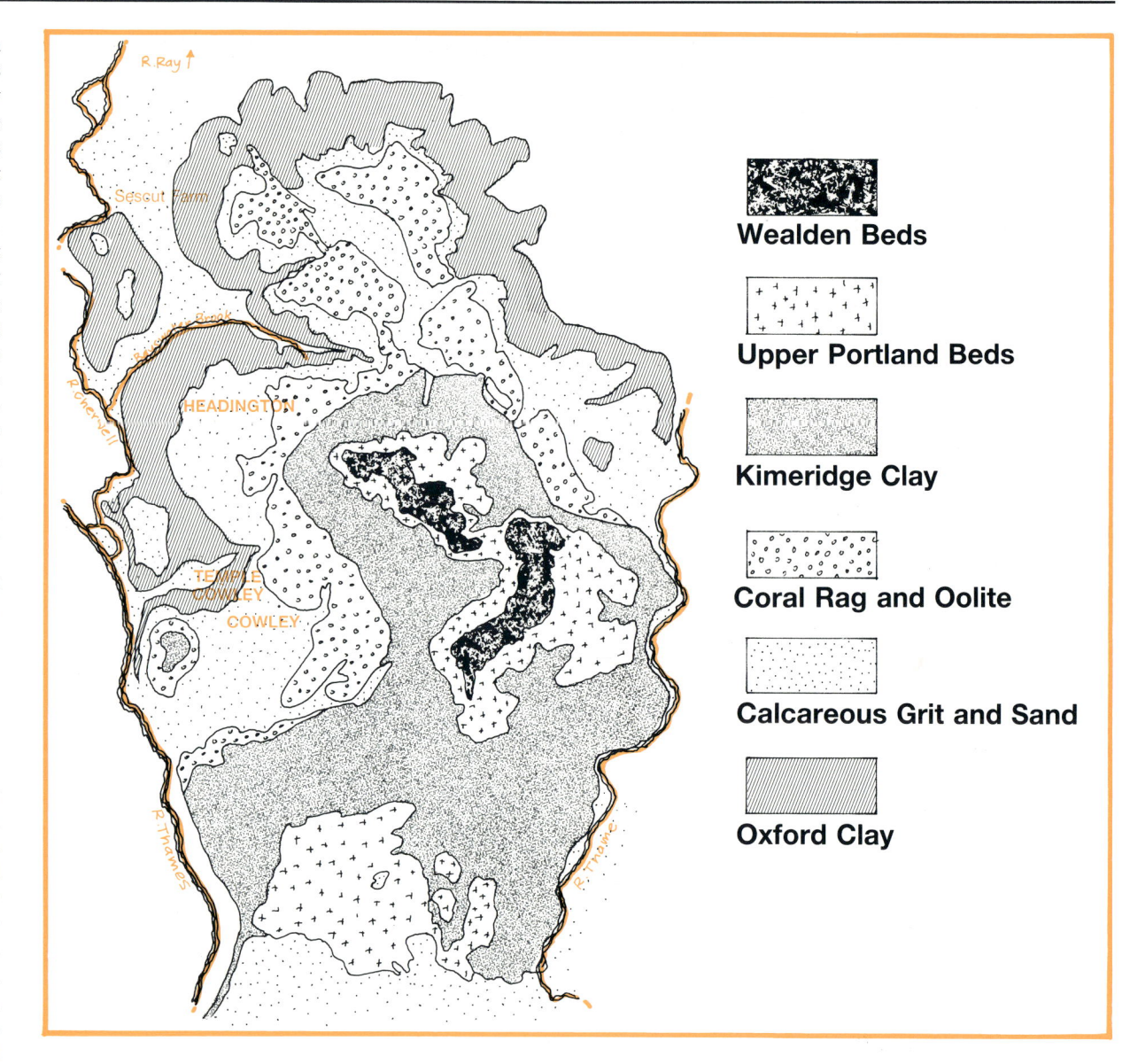

Geological Survey 1908 (reduced)

The geological ages of Oxford building stone

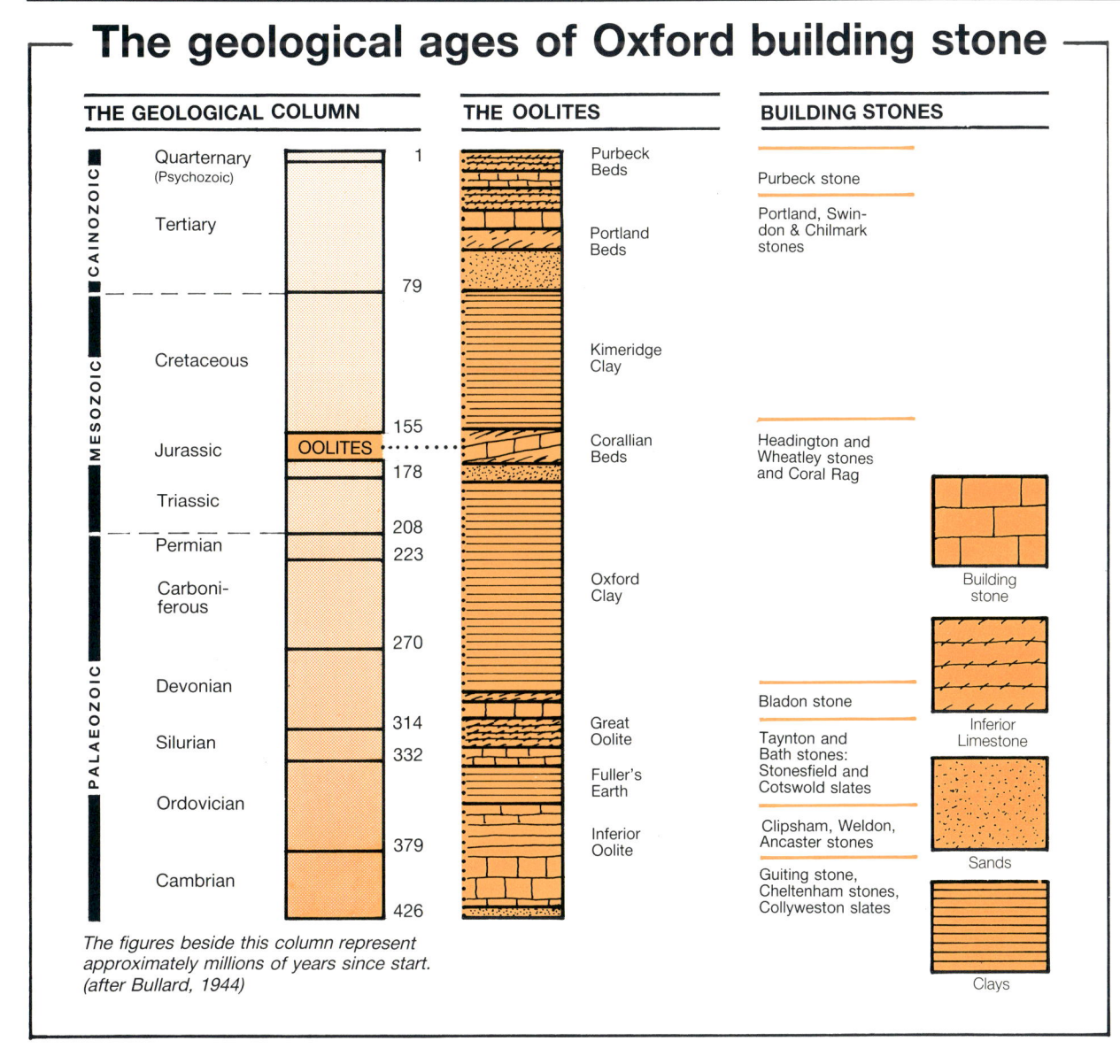

THE GEOLOGICAL COLUMN		THE OOLITES	BUILDING STONES
CAINOZOIC	Quarternary (Psychozoic) — 1	Purbeck Beds	Purbeck stone
	Tertiary — 79	Portland Beds	Portland, Swindon & Chilmark stones
MESOZOIC	Cretaceous — 155	Kimeridge Clay	
	Jurassic OOLITES — 178	Corallian Beds	Headington and Wheatley stones and Coral Rag
	Triassic — 208		
	Permian — 223	Oxford Clay	
PALAEOZOIC	Carboniferous — 270		
	Devonian — 314		Bladon stone
	Silurian — 332	Great Oolite	Taynton and Bath stones: Stonesfield and Cotswold slates
	Ordovician — 379	Fuller's Earth	Clipsham, Weldon, Ancaster stones
	Cambrian — 426	Inferior Oolite	Guiting stone, Cheltenham stones, Collyweston slates

The figures beside this column represent approximately millions of years since start. (after Bullard, 1944)

Building stone

Inferior Limestone

Sands

Clays

Based on W.J. Arkell, Oxford Stone p.30

drainage pattern took place during the Pleistocene period. The lower course of the Bayswater Brook is clearly a misfit stream, out of scale with its valley, and it seems likely that the River Ray originally flowed down the present Cherwell valley as far as Sescut Farm instead of joining the Cherwell at Islip as it does today. At the farm it turned into the broad dry valley east of Marston below Elsfield Hill, passing into the lower valley of the Bayswater Brook, and thence returning to the present course of the Cherwell, ultimately joining the Thames directly near Christ Church Meadow. At this time the Cherwell diverted from its present course near Thrupp and entered the Thames near Wolvercote. Subsequently the westward sapping of a headstream of the Ray captured the Cherwell at Thrupp, diverting this river into its present valley, and converting the Ray into a tributary. The old course of the Cherwell, left high and dry by the more rapid erosion of the valley between Thrupp and Islip, still exists between Thrupp and Wolvercote, and formed a convenient route for the construction of the Oxford Canal in the 1770s.

The geology of the Headington area

The rocks which underlie the landscape of Headington are sedimentary, laid down in shallow sea-water in a warm or even tropical climate, between 180 and 150 million years ago. They consist of oolitic limestones which alternate with deposits of thick clays and sands.

Oxford Clay underlies much of central Oxfordshire, from Bampton to near Bicester, though in the Headington area its outcrop is limited to the Bayswater Brook and Cherwell valleys. It is a thick, blue or brownish-grey clay, which usually gives rise to heavy sticky soils, though between Peasmoor Piece and Barton it is covered by a lighter loam washed down from the hills immediately to the south. Elsewhere the Oxford Clay was widely used for brick-making, but the limited outcrop in Headington does not seem to have been exploited in this way.

The Corallian beds fall into two major divisions. The distinctive series of the Lower Corallian is the Calcareous Grit, consisting of 6-9 feet (1.8-2.7m) of current-bedded brown or buff-coloured sand with a little rubbly limestone. Some 9 feet (2.7m) of sand with intermittent stone beds has been observed in cuttings beneath the road metalling of the Old High Street near the Black Boy. The soils overlying the Calcareous Grit are of a markedly sandy character.

The Upper Corallian is rather more complex. Its most consistent feature is the narrow Shell-Pebble Bed, rich in ammonite fossils, which occurs at its base. The western part of the Upper Corallian outcrop is predominantly Coral Rag, the remains of coral reefs laid down in a tropical or sub-tropical sea. This consists of 20-30 feet (6-9m) of loose, rubbly limestone with fossilized corals of both massive and branching types. Further east, towards Wheatley, the Coral Rag gives way to a detrital limestone. The change has been recorded in several of the more recently-worked quarries in Headington. In the Windmill Quarry east of the Slade 20 feet (6m) of true Coral Rag was separated from the underlying sands by the basal shell bed to the north, while in the old Crossroads Quarry east of the Wingfield Hospital a band of Coral Rag 15 feet (4.6m) deep passes laterally into broken coral beds and rubble and finally into the finely broken up coral and shell detritus. A little further to the north-east, in the Vicarage Quarry between Mark Road and Binswood Avenue, the corals are confined to a band only 6-12 inches (15-30cm) thick at the base, above which is 20 feet (6m) of nodular rubble with occasional hard bands of Wheatley

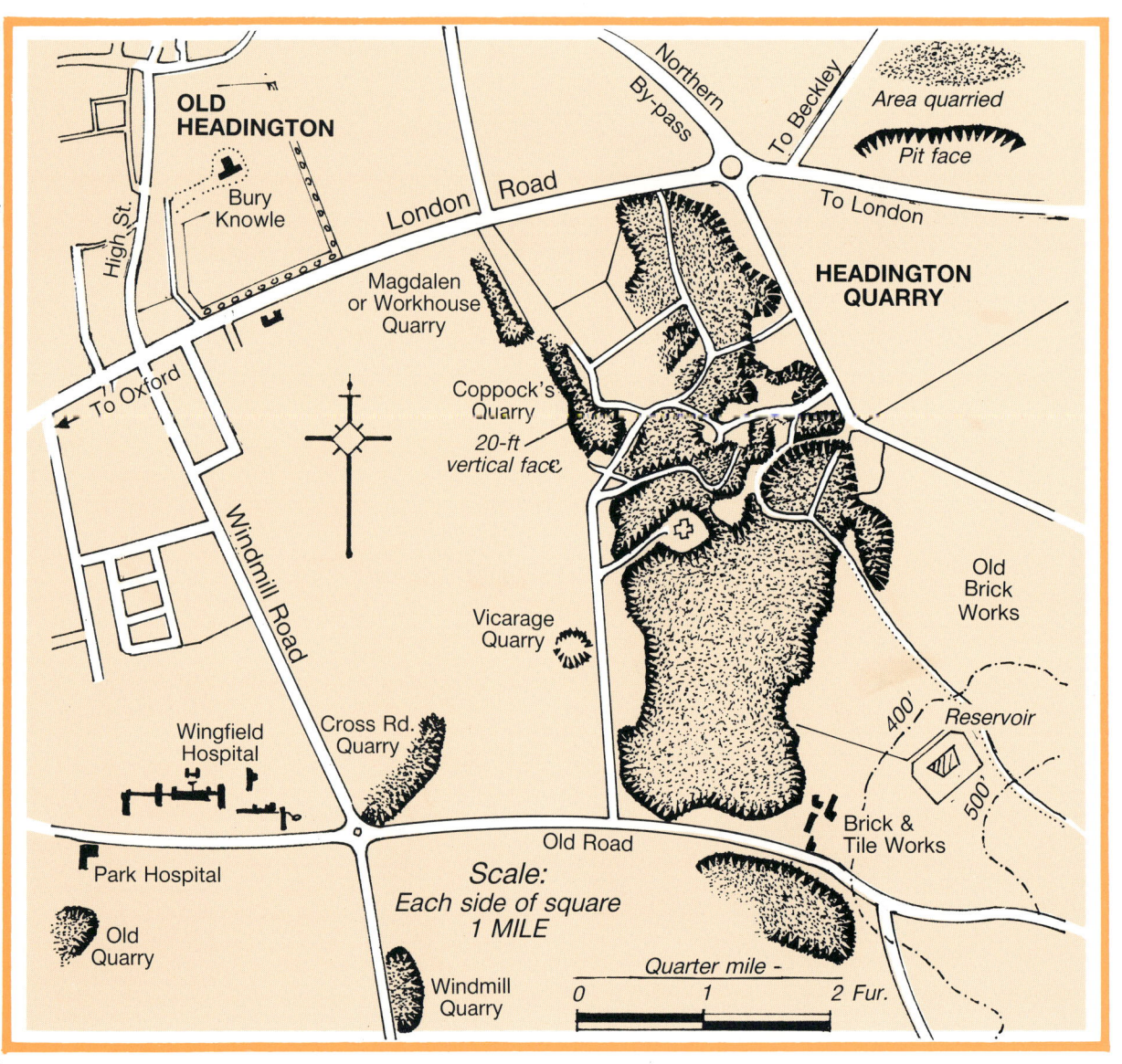

Based on W.J. Arkell, Oxford Stone p.43

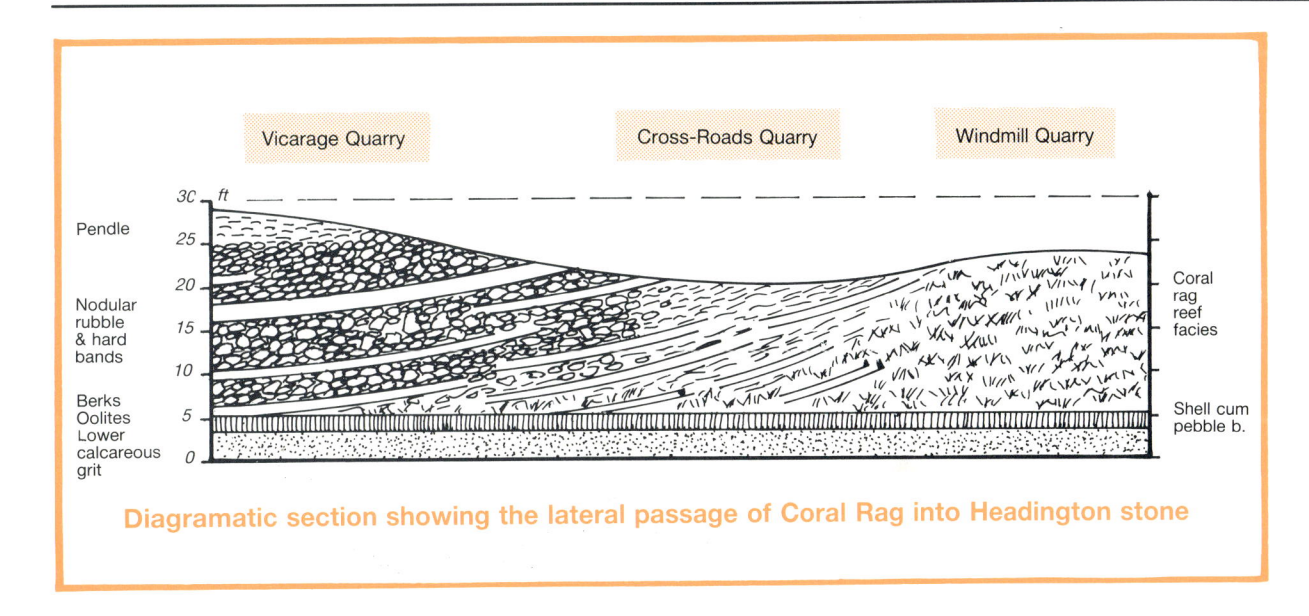

THE GEOLOGICAL AND GEOGRAPHICAL SETTING

Diagramatic section showing the lateral passage of Coral Rag into Headington stone

Based on W.J. Arkell, Oxford Stone p.45

Limestone; a similar stratification has been observed in the Workhouse or Magdalen Quarry west of Elms Road. In the Shotover quarries the Wheatley Limestone overlies the Coral Rag. Soils deriving from Coral Rag are of brashier character than those formed over the Calcareous Grit.

Building Stone

The Upper Corallian series has been of major importance as a source of building stone at least since the eleventh century, and at Headington Quarry itself the ground still bears the hummocky scars of ancient quarrying over some 90 acres (36.4 hectares). The first documentary evidence for the use of Headington stone is in the New College building accounts of 1396. The stone was used to build the bell tower, which still stands today and which has needed remarkably little renewal.

The following are some extracts from the accounts:

> For sundry iron implements weighing 127lb., bought for digging stone in Hedyndone quarry for building the tower and other walls in the college…21s. 2d.
>
> Paid to William Austyn and Hugo Glovere for baring 3 × 2 perches of Hedyndone quarry, by contract…40s.
>
> For sundry labour in the quarry at Hedyndone, digging stone for building the tower and other walls in the college…£15 15s. 11d.
>
> Paid to sundry carters for bringing 1,386 loads of stone from Hedyndone quarry to the college, etc…£23 12s. 4d.

There is also mention in these fourteenth-century accounts of lime being bought at Witney and freestone from Taynton and Barrington - the latter being used for quoins and other decorative dressings.

During the fifteenth century the lease of some of the quarry land owned by Magdalen College was held by William Orchard or Orcheyard. He was a master mason and architect and was employed by Bishop Waynflete of Winchester, who was looking after the building of Magdalen College, to build the great west window of the chapel. He completed this in 1477-8 and was then contracted for other work at Magdalen, to be built of Headington stone to be dug from the quarries belonging to the king and the college.

Two grades of stone were produced. The so-called Hardstone generally came from narrow beds of limestone, 12-18 inches (30-46cm) thick, which occurred amongst the useless rubble. This was the stone used in the walls of the bell tower at New College and it was widely used for such features as plinths and roadside curbs. The best-quality hardstone was extremely durable, and it was still being used into the middle of the nineteenth century, though some of the inferior material was liable to cavernous decay. The softer Freestone was of very local occurrence and was much more vulnerable to weathering. It was liable to crumble away through blistering and exfoliation, a process where the stone comes away in sheets or scales. This is a problem which has beset many of Oxford's buildings and helps to explain why so much re-facing has been needed. Freestone was rarely used for exterior work after the later eighteenth century, when its faults had been recognised, but it had been widely used in the preceding centuries because it was easy to work and to cut.

The Kimeridge Clay is a dark, bluish-grey clay, tending towards black near its base, with occasional sandy beds. The overall depth of the deposit is of the order of 100 feet (30m), and it underlies the northern part of the Vale of the White Horse and the north-western part of the Vale of Aylesbury. Like the Oxford Clay, it has been widely exploited for brick-making, and large brickworks were opened on the westernmost spur of Shotover Hill in the middle of the nineteenth century. The Shotover brick-pit formerly gave a good exposure of the Kimeridge beds, with 10 feet (3m) of blue-black clay containing grey calcareous nodules at the base, overlain first by the Shotover Fine Sands, a grey loamy deposit about 4 feet (1.2m) thick, then by the Shotover Grit Sands, a buff sandy deposit some 16 feet (4.9m) deep containing numerous large 'doggers' or rounded concretions. Five feet (1.5m) of grey Swindon Clay at the top was sealed by the basal pebble-bed of the overlying Portland series.

The Portland Beds, which make up most of the capping of Shotover Hill, here consist of two bands of brown-yellow and white limestone, each about two feet thick, with intervening bands of buff and mustard-coloured sand, which has been worked in the sand-pits above the Shotover brickworks. On the very top of the hill is a patch of Cretaceous rocks, the Wealden Beds, which seem to have been laid down in shallow freshwater lake conditions. These include a smooth, pale greyish-white clay which occurs on the west side of the hill, and ferruginous sands and grits which were worked for ochre during the seventeenth century and later on the southern and eastern sides of the hill.

The Portland and Wealden Beds on top of Shotover make up an example of what is known as a perched aquifer. An aquifer is a rock which can store water and through which water can flow. Here at Shotover this porous and permeable layer is overlying the impermeable Kimeridge Clay with the result that a series of springs issues along the junction line, feeding the Bayswater Brook and other streams draining eastwards towards the Thame and southwards towards the Thames. Some of the streamlets, after crossing the impermeable clay, disappear underground again in swilly holes as soon as they encounter the Coral Rag; there is a good example in the small copse between Forest Lodge and Thornhill Farm to the east of Risinghurst.

Superficial or drift deposits are not particularly significant in the Headington area. There are alluvial deposits of blue clay in the bottom of the Bayswater Brook and Cherwell valleys overlying the Oxford Clay, and also very limited narrow fingers of alluvium penetrating up the Moor Ditch and Lye Valley. River terrace gravels of the Northmoor or Floodplain terrace, 10 feet (3m) above river level, cover the Oxford Clay east of Magdalen Bridge in St Clement's but do not extend further east than London Place or Glebe Street. A rather larger patch of the Summertown-Radley terrace, some 25 feet (7.6m) above river level, covers the Oxford Clay on the southern fringes of Headington parish, south of the Cowley Road.

JAMES BOND *is an archaeologist, geographer and historian, with a particular interest in the medieval landscape.*

The past history of the village

Jean Cook and Mary Hodges

Prehistory and the Roman Period

There is only scattered archaeological evidence for the presence of man in the area of Headington in prehistoric times. There are examples of polished axes found in the parish and now in the Ashmolean and Pitt Rivers Museums. Some flint scrapers were found near Cowley Marsh and a bronze socketed spear-head was found at Sandhill, by the side of an old quarry about 250 yards north-west of Shotover Lodge.

During the Roman period it is clear that a major pottery industry was flourishing. A line of kiln sites has been found in the grounds of the Churchill Hospital and situated along, or not far from, the north-south Roman road which ran between Alchester and Dorchester, passing just to the east of Headington. The industry seems to have lasted from the second century, and possibly even from the first, to the fifth century. The kilns are actually located on an outcrop of Calcareous Grit, even though both Oxford and Kimeridge Clays occur in the close vicinity. Quite why the availability of the most bulky item of raw material did not dictate the location of the kilns more precisely is not clear. But it meant that both the clays had to be brought in for the manufacture of the red and grey coarse wares. Other materials came from even further away; white, iron-free clay for the manufacture of mortaria from the Wealden beds on top of Shotover while the grits in the mortaria bases were from the Lower Greensand, the nearest outcrops of which are at Nuneham Courtenay to the south or Cumnor Hurst and Boars Hill to the south-west.

Headington Wick (SP 549089), a site which was excavated in 1850, is best known for its villa, but the excavators also discovered evidence for the manufacture of pottery in the form of wasters and reddened earth. No pottery survives from the site and it is not now possible to decide whether its two uses, as villa and possibly as a base for making pottery, were contemporary. Harry Bear's Pit in Headington Quarry (SP 549062) lay just to the south of the point where the road from Headington village to Cowley Barracks crossed the old road from Shotover Hill. Here, in the late nineteenth century, workmen found what Percy Manning described as 'several circular hollows', probably kilns, filled with 'broken pottery, bones and dark coloured mould'. Again, none of the pottery now survives.

In Old Headington itself finds of pottery have been made over many years. In 1935 when houses were being built in Cemetery Road many potsherds were found, mostly from mortaria of pinkish-white or buff clay, dating from the late third and fourth centuries. The heavy preponderance of mortaria in this and other finds suggest the possibility of a kiln site. Judging from the wasted mortaria and kiln debris in the Ashmolean Museum, another kiln may have existed in Poor Man's Land, a site whose precise location is uncertain (probably SP 562094).

The industry must have supplied local demand but was also able to satisfy markets further away. Christopher Young has been able to demonstrate the occurrence of Oxford-made wares at a very large number of other sites - for example, one of the mortaria types, M22, associated with the Headington kilns has been found as far away as Cheshire, Devon, Humberside and Kent, as well as in Wales. Such far-flung trade reflects a well-developed market system and good communications - access to the Thames would have been relatively easy and there was an excellent road system.

Headington in Saxon times

Headington may have been at its most important in the late Saxon and Norman periods, linked - to some extent - with the growth of Oxford. During this time it was the centre of a great royal manor, whose lands covered a much larger area than that of the present parish.

Royal manors were the centres of civil government, adminstering local justice and local finance. Here the king's food-rent was paid and criminals were kept in custody. When St Frideswide founded her church in what was to become Oxford in the early part of the eighth century, the nearest centre of government would have been the manor of Headington. The land on which the monastery, almost certainly a double one for men and women, was built was probably granted from the manor's estates. The strongest piece of evidence for this is a charter of 1004 in which King Ethelred confirms the details of an endowment of land which must have been granted some time before. The charter was necessary because the original title deeds had been lost when the church of St Frideswide had been burnt down by the townspeople on the occasion of the massacre of the Danes in Oxford, ordered by the king for St Brice's day, 1002. The Danes had taken refuge in the church. Although at one time historians questioned whether this charter was genuine it is now generally accepted and this is important for the history of Headington since the charter states that it was written 'in villa regia quae vocatur Hedindona' [in the royal residence which is called Headington]. It was signed by the king and witnessed by the archbishops of Canterbury and York, Ethelred's wife, his eldest son, seven bishops, two ealdormen, four abbots and twelve thegns, suggesting that some sort of meeting - a witan or council, perhaps - had been held in the manor.

Within these walls are the possible footings of Ethelred's palace

The charter also provides evidence for the strength of the cult of St Frideswide. She had obviously been honoured as a saint for some time before 1004 - certainly long enough for her church to have been granted small manors at Cowley, Whitehill in Tackley and Cutslow; a large estate in Buckinghamshire; and the king's tithe at Headington.

The mention in the charter of a royal residence has led to speculation about the possibility of there having been a palace in Headington: there are foundations of a building of some antiquity in Ethelred Court, next to Manor Farm, marked on the 1876 Ordance Survey map as 'site of palace'. But there is no archaeological evidence to show what this building might have been. Some people have suggested a nursery for the king's children, others a hunting lodge.

Headington in Domesday Book

The next known reference to Headington is in the Domesday Book where it appears with other Oxfordshire estates as Terra Regis or land belonging to the king.

> The King holds Headington. There are 10 hides. In demesne are 6 ploughs: 20 villeins with 24 bordars have 14 ploughs.
> 2 mills at 50s; 5 fisheries at 20s; from the meadows and pastures £4; from the year's corn £8;
> from 'Helueuuecha' 30s; from church-tax 10s 6d; from other customary dues 100s and 25d.
> The Jurisdiction of two hundreds belongs to this manor; Richard de Courcy withdraws for himself (the Jurisdiction) of 16 hides.
> In total it pays £60 (a year at) face value.

It is clear that the manor was a large one - the ten hides denote an area of about 1,200 acres - but it is difficult to be certain exactly where its boundaries ran. It is likely, though, that its lands included the hamlets of Barton, Wick and Marston and may even have included outlying property in the village of Garsington. Six ploughs, each with eight oxen, were working for the king. Villeins were the most prosperous peasants, usually holding land in the village fields, whereas bordars were cottagers. The mills were water-mills. One was probably King's Mill, which stood at the point on the river Cherwell where the parishes of Headington, St. Clement's, Marston and Holywell come together. The history of this mill can be traced through various owners until it ceased working in 1832. The other mill may well have been on Bayswater Brook.

The five fisheries suggest that long stretches of the Thames and Cherwell belonged to the manor, which probably extended to the water-meadows

Extract from Domesday Book in the custody of the Public Record Office

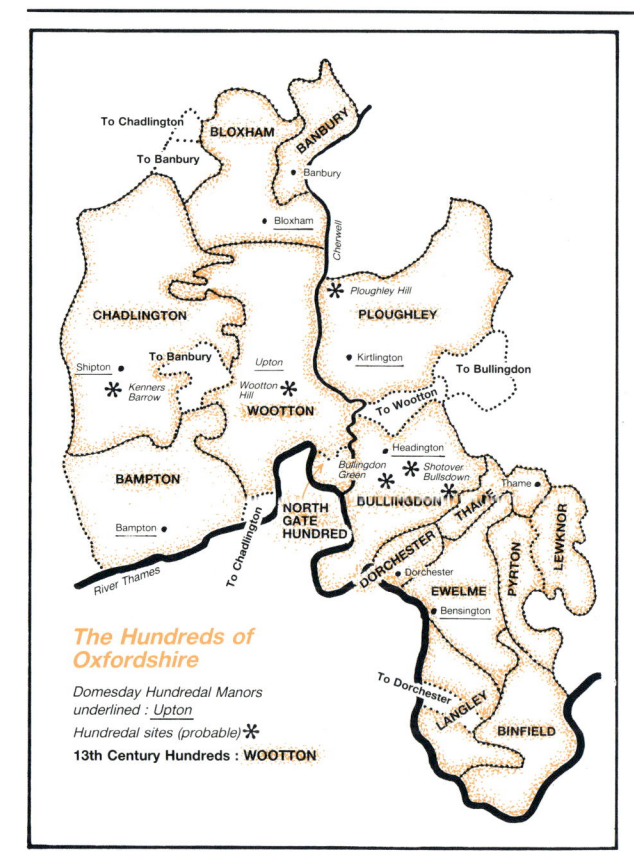

The hundreds of Oxfordshire based on Oxoniensia *Vol. I, p.116*

around Osney and Binsey. These fisheries and water-meadows were granted to various of the religious houses of Oxford, as we know from documentary evidence.

The yearly income derived from the manor came from a variety of sources as the Domesday entry shows. The sum from the year's corn was a commutation of the older corn-rents, at one time paid in kind. In the Oxfordshire Domesday entries this rent only appears in connection with royal estates and shows that they were ancient demesnes or manors belonging to the Crown during the reigns of Edward the Confessor and William I. The meaning of the word 'helueuuecha' is uncertain, though it has been suggested that it means a half-week and relates to the work service due by the week.

Another source of income was from the profits of the jurisdiction exercised in the hundreds annexed to the manor. The hundreds of Oxfordshire are not clearly defined in the Domesday survey, but two were annexed to Headington. Careful research has shown that these were Bullingdon hundred and 'the hundred outside the North Gate of Oxford'. Helen Cam has suggested that the two hundreds of Headington may have met at Bullsdown, a hill above Wheatley, in the east and at Shotover in the west, at least until the growth of the suburb to the north of the city wall meant that the meeting place had to be moved from Shotover to a site within Northgate hundred.

The early history of the Manor

The manor remained Crown property until after the death of Henry I in 1135, although by this time Woodstock had become the chief royal residence in the county. Some time before 1142 it was granted to Hugh de Pluggenait, a Breton supporter of Henry's daughter Maud. Again, we do not know the exact size of the manor at this stage, but it was valued at £42 10s, a lower sum than the £60 valuation of 1086. Even so it was still an important administrative unit, with lands extending far beyond the boundaries of Headington parish.

After Hugh's death in 1201 the manor was held by Hugh de Neville and Gilbert Bassett for short periods at its old valuation of £42 10s, but in 1203 it was granted by King John to Thomas Bassett at a yearly rent of £20. Thomas's daughter Philippa, then the widow of the Count of Warwick, succeeded to her father's estates in 1220. She then remarried, this time to Richard Siward, a man who was not a favourite of the king. He carried on various private feuds, one of which resulted in the demesne crops of Headington being seized by the king's order in 1233. Philippa died in 1265, having divorced Richard, and her estates were divided up between the co-heirs of her younger sister Alice. The husband of one of them, Hugh de Plescy, obtained the others' shares by purchase or exchange and so became the sole lord of the manor.

Hugh was not a popular man with his tenants. He tried to enforce additional labour services and so, in 1277, the men of Headington exercised their privilege as tenants of ancient demesne land to appeal to the king. The settlement, or composition, which was then made remained in force for two hundred years. Copies of it have survived and tell us a great deal about medieval Headington. Rents and services were fixed. The rent for a virgate of land was set at 10, 8 or 5 shillings, according to custom. A virgate was a measure of land, varying in size according to the quality of soil, but probably about 30 acres. Services due were set at the rate of sixteen days for one virgate and proportionally less for smaller holdings. The sixteen days were divided up:

2 days' ploughing and harrowing for the winter crop
2 days' ploughing and harrowing for the spring crop
1 day's hoeing in early summer
1 day's stirring of fallow between hay-time and harvest
2 days' mowing
1 day for turning the hay

1 day for carrying the hay to the lord's barn and stacking it
1 day reaping corn at the tenant's charge
4 days' reaping at the lord's expense
1 day gathering nuts in Stow Wood

Many other details are recorded in the composition; examples include the payment of 2s to be made when a tenant's daughter married outside the manor to compensate for the goods which she took with her, and the payment of five marks - a mark was a unit of accountancy, originally valued at 10s 8d - to the lord in lieu of paying the tax levied by the king on all his demesne land.

When Hugh's wife died in 1280, he surrendered the manor of Headington to the Crown, obtaining in exchange the manor of Long Compton in Warwickshire and the sum of £200. For the next thirty years or so the manor of Headington was administered by royal bailiffs.

In 1317 it was granted to Sir Richard Damory, who was constable of Oxford Castle and also sheriff. The rent was fixed by the Exchequer at £81, a sum which the manor was quite unable to sustain since its annual yield, leaving out the profits of jurisdiction, was £47 8s 5½d. Records tell us that in 1281 the demesne, or land belonging to the lord of the manor and farmed on his behalf, consisted of 400 acres of arable land as well as some meadow and some pasture, most of which was dispersed throughout the common fields.

Farming in medieval times

Arable land seems to have been farmed on a three-field system at this time, a system which continued until the Enclosure Award in the early nineteenth century. The three main fields were South Field, which ran down to St Bartholomew's and Cowley; Brockholes, west of the village, which sloped down towards the Cherwell; and Quarry Field, which lay to the east and south-east of the village, towards the boundary with the forest of Shotover. The problem was a shortage of good pastureland. There was little natural meadowland and what there was was rather scattered. Tenants had free pasture rights in Shotover and Stowood for pigs and cattle, and there were detailed regulations for access to stubble in cornfields, which played a vital part in the system. Numbers of livestock admitted for grazing had to be carefully controlled and even the lengths of tethering ropes had to conform.

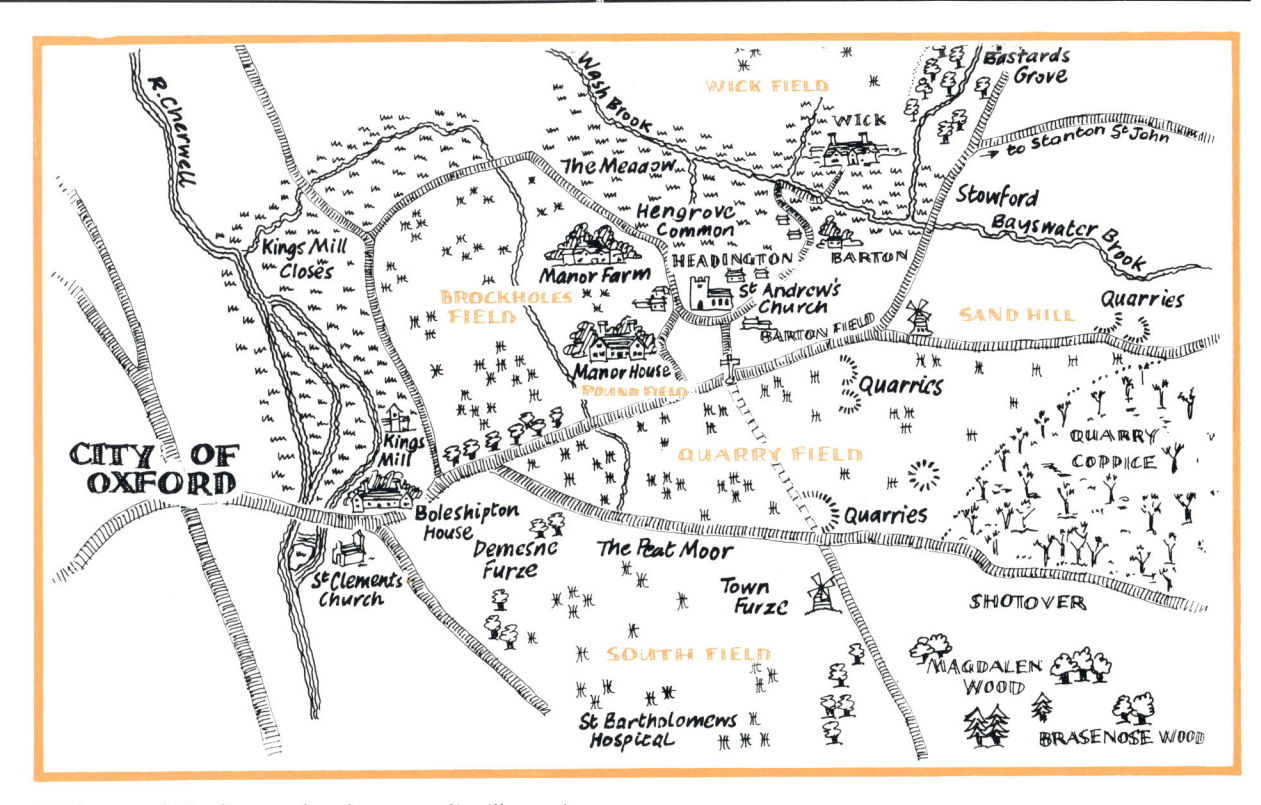

Fields around Headington, based on an earlier illustration

The Manor in the 14th and 15th centuries

When Sir Richard died his widow held a third of the manor in dower and was excused her share of the rent in recognition of her late husband's services to the king. Her son, also Sir Richard, was responsible for the remaining two-thirds, but was excused £40 of this on various conditions. By 1354 he was heavily in debt to the Crown and he had to surrender his estates to Sir John Chandos, retaining only a life tenancy. Sir John's heirs, who inherited the estate in 1375, also failed to pay their rent. The Exchequer tried to obtain livestock or other goods from the Headington tenants in lieu of this rent but was restrained from doing so and by 1399 the manor was deemed to have lapsed to the Crown.

When it was granted out again to William Willicotes of North Leigh the rent was fixed at £40. In 1401 he leased most of the demesne to St. John's Hospital and so did not need the labour services of his tenants. It is likely to have been at this period, the beginning of the fifteenth century, that the medieval manor house fell into disrepair. Neither William Willicotes nor his two sons who inherited his Headington property seem to have lived there. The estate passed through various hands until it entered the Brome family. After Ursula Brome married Sir Thomas Whorwood they lived for a time in Headington, at Mason's Farm because the manor house no longer existed.

Sir Thomas was another aggressive landlord and it is known that in James I's reign the tenants again invoked their ancient demesne privilege of appeal to the king; unfortunately this case has not been traced. Sir Thomas was still paying the rent of £40 a year fixed in 1399, although by the early seventeenth century the receipts from Headington and the other family seat of Holton were estimated at £1,000. On the death of his father-in-law, John Brome, in 1613 the Exchequer questioned the validity of his claim to the title of the Headington estates in an attempt to repossess the land for the Crown. This attempt did not succeed, however, and the property remained in the possession of the Whorwood family.

Headington Quarry

The importance of Headington stone has already been mentioned. The beginning of Quarry hamlet, marking the first evidence of any permanent

One of the old quarries in Quarry village (Oxfordshire County Libraries)

Headington Quarry (Oxfordshire County Libraries)

General Fairfax outside Oxford, taken from An Impartial History of the Rebellion and Civil Wars in England *by Jacob Hooper, 1738 (Bodleian library, Fol. θ 174)*

settlement round the sites of the quarries, dates from the early years of the seventeenth century, when the quarries were at the height of their prosperity. Several Oxford colleges owned quarries, among them Magdalen, Corpus Christi, All Souls, Christ Church, Oriel, Balliol, Queen's and Lincoln. Sir Thomas Whorwood was vexed to find that little of the profit from the quarries accrued to him as lord of the manor, and so a ruling was made in the manorial court that the colleges were not freehold owners but copyholders, implying the payment of dues. He also had new pits dug for his own exploitation. The Exchequer, ever eager to increase the Crown revenue, tried to prove that the new pits were outside the parish boundary and within that of the forest, but this does not seem to have come to much.

The fact that so may colleges had a direct interest in the quarries meant that the link between the village and the University was a strong one. Headington was already a favourite place to visit on the part of undergraduates, who frequented the ale-houses such as Joan of Headington's, Widow Coxe's and Mother Gurdon's. Bull-baiting was a well-known sport and in 1727 there was one occasion when undergraduates, who had been prevented by the villagers from tying a cat to the bull's tail, retaliated by smashing windows and breaking into houses. It took the arrival of the proctors to restore order. The villagers themselves were not always law-abiding. During the fifteenth and sixteenth centuries they apparently refused to confine themselves to practising archery for exercise but preferred 'illoyal games' i.e. ball games and a bowling alley, both of which caused disturbance of the peace and required the manorial court to sort matters out.

Headington in the Civil War

During the Civil War Headington was of considerable strategic importance, because of its topographical position, commanding the eastern approaches to Oxford. It was occupied by the royalists in 1643 and in 1645 it became a look-out post for the parliamentary party. Later General Fairfax moved his headquarters there from Marston, billeting his troops in the village and establishing a free market in an attempt to prevent produce from being taken down into Oxford to relieve the royalist garrison stationed there in St Clement's.

The Enclosure Award

In 1880 the manors of Headington and Holton were put up for sale, but for some reason the Headington sale did not go forward. Henry Mayne Whorwood was in residence at the Manor House, a replacement for the medieval one, at the time of the Enclosure Award in 1804. The Act of Parliament for the enclosure of the open fields of Headington parish was passed in 1802 and the award itself was managed by Richard Davis of Lewknor and John Davis of Bloxham together with Edward Barton of Headington as Commissioners of the Act. The Davises were surveyors and land agents who dealt with the business aspects of the award, but Edward Barton was a beneficiary to the extent of just over four acres, as was his wife Martha. In all forty-two people became land-owners as a result of the award.

Henry Whorwood may, together with the other major land-owners of the time, have been part of the movement for enclosure, the purpose of which was to reorganise the land of the parish from the number of small strips scattered widely within open fields to a series of smaller, hedged fields, with property belonging to one individual grouped in one area. The opportunity was taken to enclose some 'waste' land at the same time, since even this could be profitable. It has been suggested that one of the main motivating forces may have been that of property development and the Whorwood family certainly had plans to extend the estate to include 'a crescent and detached villas in the best style'. Even so, farming continued to be the main occupation in the parish for many years; there were still five active farms in existence in 1891.

The Enclosure Award gives details of the major land-owners in the village at the time. Henry

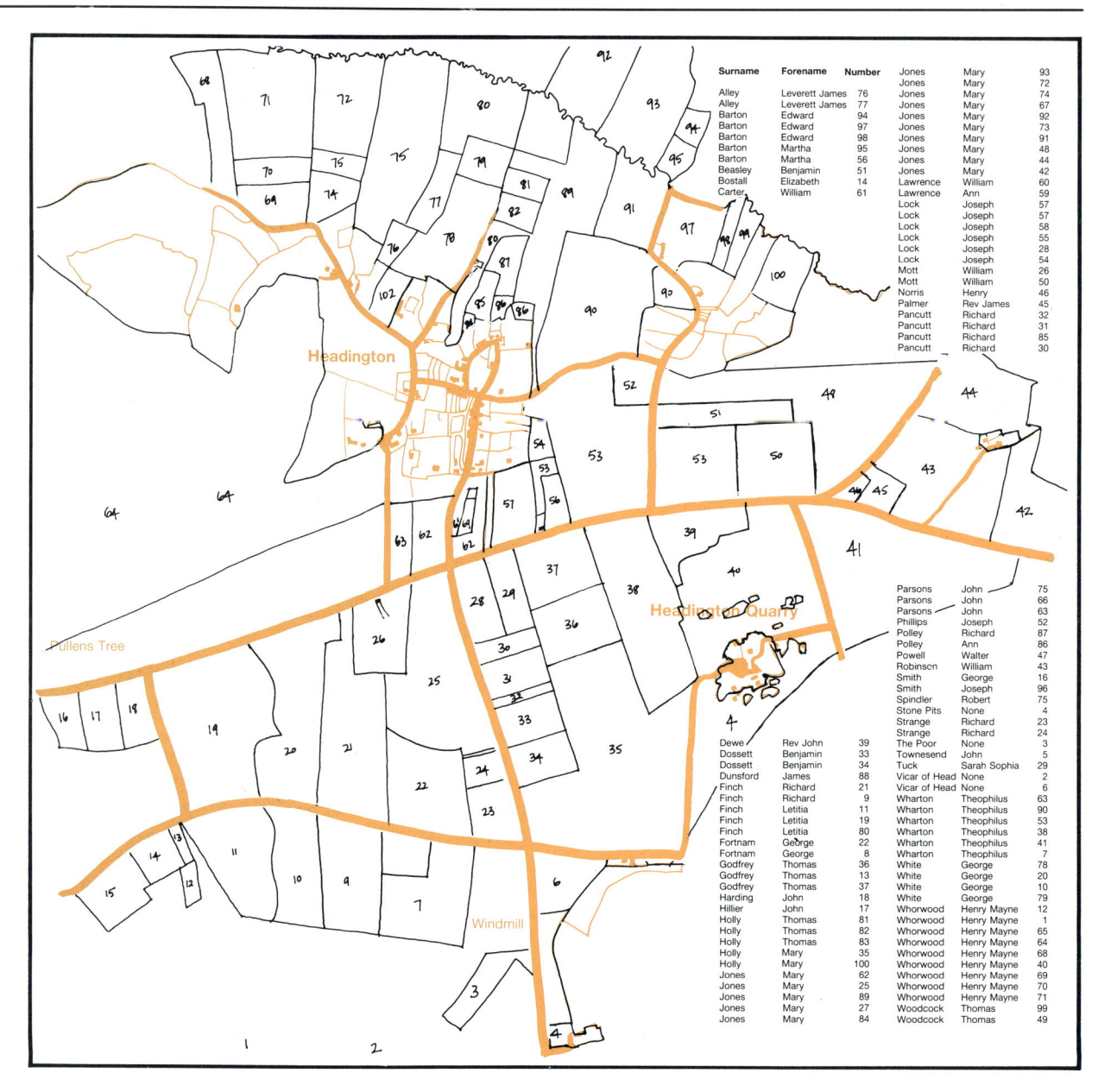

Surname	Forename	Number
Alley	Leverett James	76
Alley	Leverett James	77
Barton	Edward	94
Barton	Edward	97
Barton	Edward	98
Barton	Martha	95
Barton	Martha	56
Beasley	Benjamin	51
Bostall	Elizabeth	14
Carter	William	61
Dewe	Rev John	39
Dossett	Benjamin	33
Dossett	Benjamin	34
Dunsford	James	88
Finch	Richard	21
Finch	Richard	9
Finch	Letitia	11
Finch	Letitia	19
Finch	Letitia	80
Fortnam	George	22
Fortnam	George	8
Godfrey	Thomas	36
Godfrey	Thomas	13
Godfrey	Thomas	37
Harding	John	18
Hillier	John	17
Holly	Thomas	81
Holly	Thomas	82
Holly	Thomas	83
Holly	Mary	35
Holly	Mary	100
Jones	Mary	62
Jones	Mary	25
Jones	Mary	89
Jones	Mary	27
Jones	Mary	84
Jones	Mary	93
Jones	Mary	72
Jones	Mary	74
Jones	Mary	67
Jones	Mary	92
Jones	Mary	73
Jones	Mary	91
Jones	Mary	48
Jones	Mary	44
Jones	Mary	42
Lawrence	William	60
Lawrence	Ann	59
Lock	Joseph	57
Lock	Joseph	57
Lock	Joseph	58
Lock	Joseph	55
Lock	Joseph	28
Lock	Joseph	54
Mott	William	26
Mott	William	50
Norris	Henry	46
Palmer	Rev James	45
Pancutt	Richard	32
Pancutt	Richard	31
Pancutt	Richard	85
Pancutt	Richard	30
Parsons	John	75
Parsons	John	66
Parsons	John	63
Phillips	Joseph	52
Polley	Richard	87
Polley	Ann	86
Powell	Walter	47
Robinson	William	43
Smith	George	16
Smith	Joseph	96
Spindler	Robert	75
Stone Pits	None	4
Strange	Richard	23
Strange	Richard	24
The Poor	None	3
Townsend	John	5
Tuck	Sarah Sophia	29
Vicar of Head	None	2
Vicar of Head	None	6
Wharton	Theophilus	63
Wharton	Theophilus	90
Wharton	Theophilus	53
Wharton	Theophilus	38
Wharton	Theophilus	41
Wharton	Theophilus	7
White	George	78
White	George	20
White	George	10
White	George	79
Whorwood	Henry Mayne	12
Whorwood	Henry Mayne	1
Whorwood	Henry Mayne	65
Whorwood	Henry Mayne	64
Whorwood	Henry Mayne	68
Whorwood	Henry Mayne	40
Whorwood	Henry Mayne	69
Whorwood	Henry Mayne	70
Whorwood	Henry Mayne	71
Woodcock	Thomas	99
Woodcock	Thomas	49

The Old Manor House, now part of the John Radcliffe Hospital (Oxfordshire County Libraries)

The old pathway to the churchyard

Whorwood owned about 565 acres freehold, leasing a further 19 or so from Corpus Christi. Mary Jones owned some 51 acres freehold, 58 as a copyholder of the manor and 91 on lease from Magdalen College. Most of the rest of the people listed were either copyholders of land on the manor estate or held it on lease from Magdalen, making the college and the lord of the manor the two biggest land-owners. Joseph Lock, who was a goldsmith and banker with premises in High Street, Oxford, held 16 acres as a copyholder to the manor. As a result of the enclosure of his land, in particular one field, the footpath from Quarry hamlet to the church was closed. The minutes of the Commissioners' committee meeting on 10 January 1803 read:

> we also considered an application made at several former meetings by Mr Lock respecting a footpath which now passes in a diagonal manner across the Allotment in front of his house and directed our surveyor to make such alteration therein as appeared to be proper and necessary.

This path had been used by people carrying coffins from Quarry to St Andrew's Church for burial and to go to church before 1850; it seems to have been the still existing path behind the present International Stores and car-park. At the next funeral Mr Lock's new wall was broken down. The Whorwoods, one of whom was the lord of the manor and the other, his brother, the vicar, were - not surprisingly - on the side of the land-owner, but the curate, James Palmer, took up the cause of Quarry villagers. Palmer, when threatened with dismissal, appealed to the Bishop who ruled that he must not be dismissed unless the vicar, who was living elsewhere, came into residence and that, in the meantime, the curate's stipend should be increased from £27 10s (on which he had to find his own house and support his wife and two children) to £35. The vicar did in fact come into residence; his brother died in 1806 and so he became lord of the manor.

The parish duties were not particularly onerous at the time. The only regular services were morning and evening prayer on Sundays, with one sermon. Communion services were much less frequent, the sacrament being administered on average three times a year. In the 1820s the number of communicants was between 40 and 50. By 1808 a Sunday School had been started and in 1850 the ecclesiastical parish of Headington Quarry was created.

The end of the Manor

The Whorwood estate was offered for sale in lots, in 1849 the manor farm and the manorial rights were sold to the trustees of William Peppercorn and the manor house was bought a year or so earlier by a solicitor, John Matthews. His wife sold it in 1858 and it was eventually bought in 1895 by Colonel James Hoole, CMG. Colonel Hoole was able to purchase the manor farm and the manorial rights from William Peppercorn's heirs in 1906 and so the estate was once again united. It was bought in 1917 by the trustees of the Radcliffe Infirmary as a site for development at some future date.

Headington and the 1851 Census

Apart from the Enclosure Award, 1801 also saw the beginning of the census system. Information was collected every ten years, using much the same method as is used today. The job of the local census enumerator was to copy the information provided by individual householders onto official forms which made up the census enumerator's books from 1851 onwards. Details had to be provided on the age, sex, marital status, occupation and place of birth of everyone present in the house on the census night. For the local historian this information is invaluable and it becomes available for study one hundred years after the census was taken. The census enumerator's books for Headington for 1851 and 1881 provide a fascinating picture of life in the second half of the nineteenth century.

Barton village road early this century: Barton Manor can be seen beyond the brick building

At the time of the census the enumerator went to great trouble to describe the areas within the parish of Headington. He identified Headington St Andrew's, Headington Quarry (Holy Trinity after 1849), Barton, Headington Hill, the Warneford Lunatic Asylum, the Poor Law Union Workhouse -

The remaining oasis of Bartlemas off the Cowley Road (Oxfordshire County Libraries)

Headington was the centre of a Poor Law Union which included twenty-four surrounding parishes - and the extra-parochial area of Bartlemas. His descriptions had to include information on the city and parliamentary boundaries. For example, in 1881 he describes district 6 as follows:

All that remaining part of Headington Parish which lies on the North side of London Road to the east of Rose Cottage, corner of Sandy Lane comprising the Manor House and farm, cottages in the meadows, Headington village, Barton Wick Farm, Wiggins Farm, Sandhill, Windmill Hill and Parochial Schools on the south side of London Road all being within the ecclesiastical district of St Andrew's and within the Headington Rural Sanitary District.

Such a careful description and the division of the whole area into districts makes it possible to single out Old Headington.

The following table shows the overall totals of people living in what is now Old Headington at the time of the two censuses.

	Place of birth Headington		Place of birth Oxfordshire		Place of birth outside Oxfordshire		
	Men	Women	Men	Women	Men	Women	Total
1851	267	214	88	138	22	58	787
%	33.93%	27.19%	11.19%	17.53%	2.80%	7.37%	
total %	61.12%		28.72%		10.17%		
1881	298	272	89	134	45	69	907
%	32.86%	29.99%	9.81	14.77	4.96	7.61	
total %	62.84%		24.59%		12.57%		

We can pick out various points from such a table. The increase in the adult population over the thirty years is 120; this compares with the increase in the total adult population of the parish from 1,668 in 1841 to 3,696 in 1901, suggesting that the parish as a whole was growing faster than the village, which was changing relatively little. The village population was also very stable; 61% of those accounted for in the 1851 census and almost 63% of those in the 1881 census had been born in the village. It is also clear that in both cases a higher proportion of women were born outside the village or outside the county. This is not unusual; the women generally came to Headington as wives or to work as servants.

Village occupations

It is possible to see how the villagers made their livings by looking at the information in the census returns; 102 separate occupations were listed in 1851 and 76 in 1881. There were substantial groups working in agriculture - 49 agricultural labourers in 1851 and 47 in 1881. Four farmers appear in both censuses and three farm bailiffs also. The five market gardeners of 1851 had been reduced to two by 1881, but ten gardeners in 1851 had become twenty thirty years later; they may have been working in Oxford, perhaps in the colleges. The numbers involved in the building trade grew over the thirty years in question - fourteen carpenters but no bricklayers in 1851, whereas by 1881 there were 15 bricklayers and 8 builders' labourers as well as a builder. Carpenters were reduced to nine, but one of them was also a musician. In 1881 a row of eight newly completed but unoccupied houses were listed by the enumerator, reflecting the building boom which must have occurred in Oxford and its immediate environs in the period after 1870. Men who were listed simply as labourers numbered 20 in 1851 and 49 by 1881; they may have been involved in building. The quarry provided work for one quarryman and five others doing various stone-quarrying jobs in 1851, but by 1881 there was only one man in Old Headington connected directly with the quarry and he declares himself to be a stone quarry manager. However there were in the later census four masons and fourteen masons' labourers, so no doubt skills in stone were being transferred to the building trade.

Women's occupations included shopkeeping and butchery for a few, but sixteen laundresses in 1851 had risen to thirty-seven by 1881. They were almost certainly involved in taking in college laundry. Eighteen dressmakers and needlewomen 1881 also reflect an increase over the thirty years.

Thirty-one servants were listed in 1851 and seventy-six in 1881, of whom sixty-four were women.

Somewhat more unusual were the group of wood-engravers in 1851, four of them as well as an apprentice; by 1881 they had disappeared, steel-engraving having replaced their trade, but three printers and compositors had replaced them. The usual range of trades and crafts reflecting Headington's independent status included wheelwright, blacksmith, whitesmith, seven bakers, various shops and butchers and even, by 1881, a fruiterer and florist. The one carrier of 1851 was joined by another by 1881.

It is easy to see that although the size of the community changes little over the thirty years an increasing prosperity is apparent. In 1851 thirty-seven people were declared as either paupers or on parish relief, but by 1881 there was no-one in this group. A possible explanation is that some in this category may by then have entered the workhouse in the Quarry. Those of higher status included several annuitants and pensioners and by 1881 there were twenty-six people in the professional and independent class in the village. Even the pleasant occupation of cricketer appears in 1851, and then in 1881 that of professional bowler!

Size of households

The average size of households in the village in 1851 was 4.64 people. This dropped marginally by 1881 to 4.34. However, this average conceals the large families we expect in the nineteenth century - Mr and Mrs Kimber (Elias and Caroline), who ran the Prince's Castle public house in Barton in 1881 and were aged 32 and 33 respectively, had eight children aged from 11 years to 5 months - five sons and three daughters. In the same census was Miss Isabella Watson-Taylor, aged 66, living at the Manor House. She declared her income as coming from dividends and she had seven servants living in the house - a butler, cook, lady's maid, house-maid, kitchen-maid and two stable boys. William Wootten-Wootten of Headington House, a banker aged 59 with his wife Sarah aged 57, had six unmarried children living at home: Eliza aged 29, Montague 28, Gilbert 24, Alice 23, Edward 21 and Katherine 19 - none of them with any stated occupation. Looking after them were a cook, nurse and house-maid.

Children in the 19th century

The information in the two censuses about children under fourteen years of age is summarised in the following table.

	At home		At school		At work		
	Male	Female	Male	Female	Male	Female	Total
1851	85	101	46	61	12	2	307
%	27.69	32.90	14.98	19.87	3.91	0.65	
total %	60.59		34.85		4.56		
1881	42	32	110	121	10	10	325
%	12.92	9.85	33.85	37.23	3.08	3.08	
total %	22.77		71.08		6.15		

From this we can see that only 107 of the 307 children were at school in 1851, according to the census use of the term 'Scholar'. Fourteen of them were at work, the girls as servants and the boys as farm labourers or errand boys. According to the 1881 census 231 children in the village were 'scholars' and twenty were at work - still as servants and errand boys, though one boy of 13 was a solicitor's clerk.

Mrs. Morrell's Training School for Servants on the site of Oxford Polytechnic (Oxfordshire County Libraries)

Schools

There seem to have been two schools in the 1850s. One was the so-called Free School with James Waring and his wife as teachers - he was also the postmaster. This school had 12 boys and 12 girls and was probably the only one left of the group of five small fee-paying schools which existed in the village in 1833. The title Free may have referred to its religious affiliation. The Warings were still at the school in 1869.

There was also a National School, the direct descendant of a school founded by the bequest of the interest on £400 left by Catherine Mather in 1805 for educating 6 poor boys and 6 poor girls. A panel on the south wall of the Baptistry in St Andrew's Church commemorates this bequest and the school started off in the Chequers Inn. To return to the National School, this had recently - probably in 1851 - moved into new premises, the red brick Gothic-styled building now part of St Andrew's First School. It had 85 boys and 85 girls and the headmaster was John Bird. His wife also taught at the school. Miss Ann Bird (a daughter?), was in charge of the newly established Infants' School for 60 children, which was supported by private subscriptions. We can pick up the names of the headmasters of the National School from directories; Henry Franklin by 1863, Mr Vallis in 1869, Thomas Yeates by 1876, by which time Mary Ann Crozier was in charge of the Infants' School. The Headington Quarry National School had been founded by 1877 and David Marshall was headmaster. George Stace had become headmaster of Headington National School in 1879 and held the post until 1921, when his son George succeeded him and remained as headmaster until 1952.

Certainly the expanding provision of school places had resulted in a strong move into school even before education was free. A new Church of England school was built in 1894 to accommodate the increasing population of New Headington. It was designed for 260 children and was built in front of the old National School, which then became the Infants' department which had previously been in premises at North Place. The Infants' school in New Headington continued with Miss Price as head and an average of 54 children there. In 1895 the Quarry National School had Alfred Bickley as headmaster and two assistant teachers - Miss Shepherd and Miss Rogers - while Miss Higgs was in charge of the infants. By 1907 the Quarry school had places for 161 children and a further 135 infants; the National School at Headington had 284 children, with 61 at the New Headington Infants' School. In this year, 1907, the Mather Foundation was changed to provide an exhibition to a public secondary school and in 1908 a new Council school was built for 370 children in Margaret Road - the present Windmill First School.

Apart from these schools the village also had its

fair share of other educational establishments. In 1851 Miss Mary Hanwell ran a Ladies' Seminary for five pupils aged from 11 to 13 years old. She had one assistant teacher to help her - surely a highly favourable teacher/pupil ratio! Miss Ann Weller appears in the 1854 Directory as a schoolmistress - perhaps she was Miss Hanwell's assistant. In the 1881 census a boys' preparatory school was run at the Rookery by the Rev John Augustus Taylor, a widower aged 63, an MA and a clergyman 'without cure of souls'. Also living at the Rookery were his daughter Sarah Louisa, aged 37, who was an artist and painter in oils, and his son Arthur, aged 17, both unmarried. Staying with them at the time of the census was Mrs Lucinda Bartlett, a widow aged 53 from Drayton in Oxfordshire, with her maid. There were nine boy boarders aged from 10 to 15. Looking after the household were five servants: a manservant of 62, the cook aged 26, two house maids and a kitchenmaid.

By 1887 Dr Walter Sumner Gibson had taken over the Rookery school but he is no longer listed in the Directory of 1907. By 1895 Mrs Morrell's Training Home for Servants had been founded with Miss Drake in charge, while Miss Steff's kindergarten school at 41 St Andrew's Road was certainly in existence before 1891. From here the children went on to the Infants' school, situated in North Place until its move in 1894. This school had been taken over after the 1870 Education Act, but remained a church foundation and Mrs Ballachey, who had run the school as a private enterprise, continued to contribute £20 a year to its upkeep.

Allotments

The demand for allotments gathered momentum towards the end of the nineteenth century. When Headington fields were enclosed in 1802 this brought ownership of land into the hands of comparatively few people. The state of the 'labouring poor', a phrase used in Government reports, urged some reformers to propose that some land in the parish should be set aside to be cultivated in small plots by the labourers. These small plots, or 'allotments', could be as large as a quarter of an acre and here men would grow wheat and barley for sale. In Headington in 1876 allotments 'for the use of sober and industrious labourers' were established on a field which had belonged to the vicar at the time of the enclosure; it was situated at the crossing of Old Road and Windmill Road. Not long after in 1880 the Headington Horticultural, Cottage Garden and Poultry Society was founded and held an annual show of produce. This development coincides with the establishment of the British Workman in Old High Street - a temperance club to encourage the same sober and industrious labourers for whom the allotments were intended.

JEAN COOK *is an editor and part-time tutor in archaeology and local history for Oxford University Department for External Studies.*

MARY HODGES *is a historian and part-time tutor in local history and computing for Oxford University Department for External Studies.*

The south face of St. Andrew's Churchyard cross, based on architect's drawing by Robert Maguire, 1960

The parish church

Julian Munby

St Andrew's Church stands at the heart of the village of Old Headington. It may have originated before the Norman Conquest as the chapel of the royal manor at Headington. Certainly the canons of the Priory of St Frideswide seem to have enjoyed the tithes of the manor from the time of Ethelred. This is borne out by the first documentary reference to the church which is in a charter of Henry I, dating from 1122 and granting the 'chapel' at Headington to the canons of St Frideswide's at the time of the latter's re-foundation. The chapel was to be free of all custom due to the bishop and archdeacon, and since this could only be claimed if the parish was already exempt at the time of appropriation it seems that this must have been so. This in turn suggests that Henry's charter may have been confirmation of what already existed. Certainly when the claim to exemption from episcopal control was challenged in 1232 it was said to have been in existence for a very long time, and the commissioners conducting the enquiry confirmed the validity of the claim. It seems finally to have lapsed some time during the sixteenth century.

The canons held the living, taking the tithes in their capacity as rector of the church. Initially the church was served by a chaplain, but the canons established a vicarage there in 1222 under pressure from Bishop Hugh of Lincoln. The vicar was to live in the house previously occupied by the chaplain and was allowed to have only the small tithes and the offerings of the altar. He was not granted any share of the glebe - land normally offered to the incumbent as part of the benefice - and the tithe of lambs and the tithe of cheese from the manor estates were withheld for the Priory of St Frideswide. The vicar's total emoluments were valued at a quarter of the value of the church as a whole, so the rest made up a valuable source of income for the Priory.

The office of vicar survived until 1451, though still with its meagre endowment, when St Frideswide's obtained authority to amalgamate it with the vicarage of Marston because the parishes were deemed too poor to support two priests. So one curate was appointed to serve both parishes, and this situation continued up to 1526. On the dissolution of St Frideswide's, possession of the living of Headington passed to Cardinal College, the college founded by Henry VIII, and then to its successor, Christ Church, who held it in 1535. The joint rectories of Marston and Headington were then estimated to be worth £12 and the living at Headington a mere £3. In 1545 Christ Church then sold the living to some London merchants who, in turn, sold it to the lord of the manor in 1547. This did little to improve the situation, though the curate appointed by the lord of the manor was no longer responsible for Marston as well as Headington. One curate, John Horne, a fellow of Oriel College, successfully re-established his claim to the lesser tithes but he obviously had difficulty in collecting them. Eventually, in 1680, the endowment of the living was permanently restored. Although the vicar still had no share of the glebe he was entitled to tithes of garden and orchard produce and of lambs, pigs and calves from the demesne land as well as from the rest of the parish.

Even this did not mean that the parish now had resident vicars. Many of them were fellows of Oxford colleges, living in Oxford, who sometimes appointed curates to relieve them of their parish duties. The vicar's house, consisting of two cottages with an orchard and close next to the churchyard, fell into disrepair so that even the curate could not be expected to live there and he obtained a licence to live in Oxford.

At the turn of the century

Early in the nineteenth century, at the time of the Enclosure Award, the lay rector - who was, of course, also the lord of the manor - was awarded 220 acres of land in lieu of rectorial tithes, and the vicar, who was not only the brother of the lord of the manor but was also not even resident in the parish at the time, received 96 acres. Neither of these men found much favour with the villagers. The lord of the manor, Henry Mayne Whorwood, was described as having led a very debauched life, some of it in Germany, so that he had

imbibed notions so contrary to all religion and everything resembling it that he does not scruple to call it all priestcraft.

His brother, it was felt, could not

differ from him materially without danger of starvation.

These two men were involved in an issue arising out of the Enclosure Award which has already been described previously in an earlier section on page 18.

The living remained in the gift of the Whorwood family until at least 1883, after which it passed through various hands until it was acquired by Keble College in 1928.

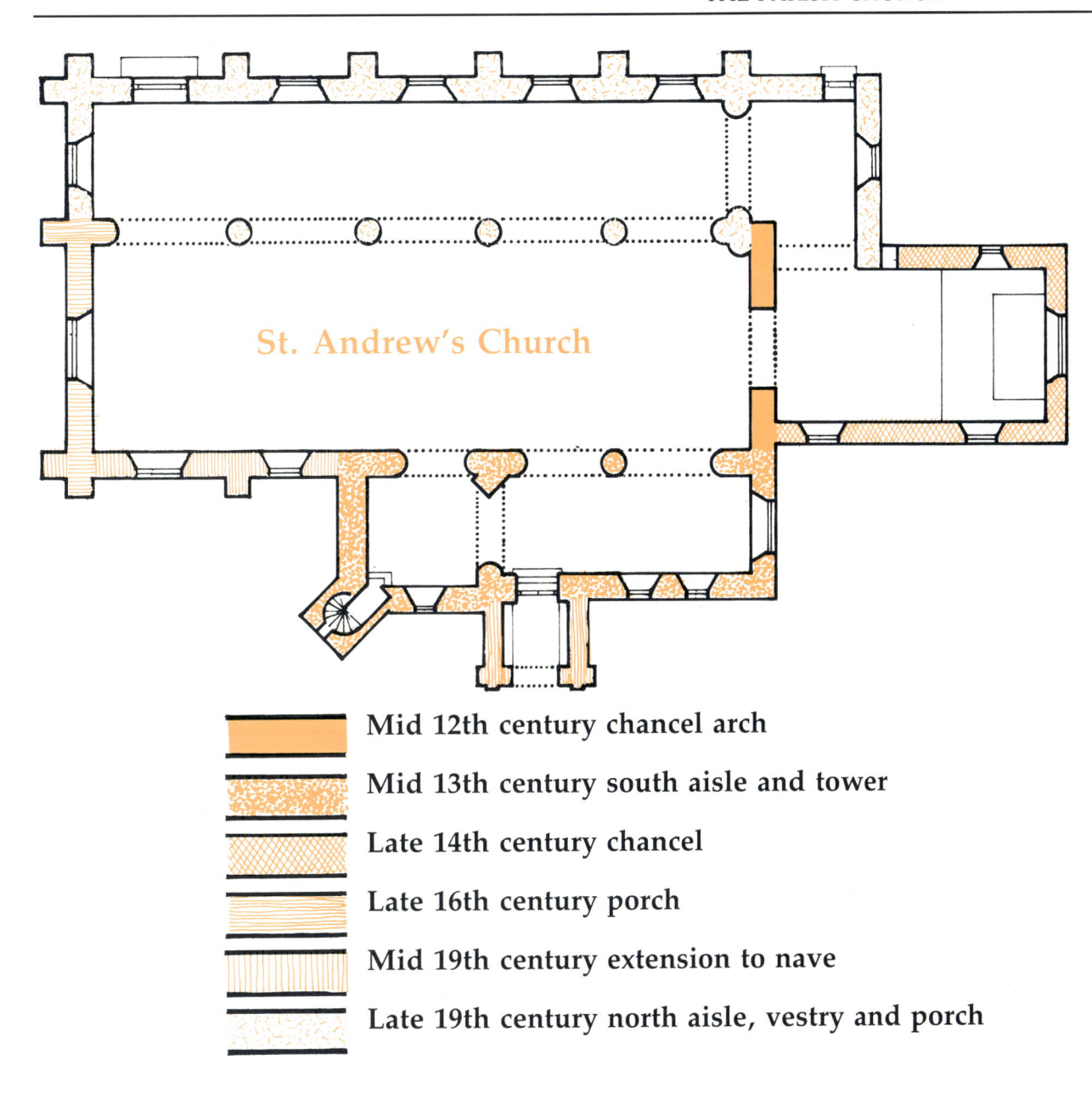

The history of the Church buildings

The romanesque chancel arch, built in the mid-twelfth century of local stone, still survives. This formed part of what was probably the first stone church on the site, though this may have replaced one or more earlier buildings, possibly made of wood. This early stone church consisted of nave and chancel, the nave extending westwards a few feet beyond the present tower arch. It may have been built by the lord of the manor at the time, Sir Hugh de Pluggenait. He is recorded as a generous benefactor to St Frideswide's Priory, partly as the result of the healing of one of his kinsmen at the saint's shrine. Certainly he endowed an altar lamp for St Andrew's Church to mark his gratitude.

In the mid-thirteenth century a fine south aisle was added to the church, with lancet windows in both east and south walls, and with an arcade of two bays leading across to the nave. The east end of this aisle formed the Lady Chapel. The jambs of the windows on the south side were decorated with wall-paintings, also of thirteenth-century date, which portrayed the flight of the Holy Family into Egypt, a favourite legend of the period. In the corner of one of the panels was the figure of a kneeling lady, the donor of the Chapel. It is thought that this represents Philippa, widow of the Count of Warwick, who succeeded to the manor in 1220 and occupied it until 1265.

The arch of about the same date to the base of the tower suggests that there may have been a south tower at that time, whilst a similar arch was built over the original chancel arch to give it support.

By the end of the fourteenth century the chancel was rebuilt, the work being carried out under the auspices of St Frideswide's Priory in its capacity as rector. The windows in the north and south walls

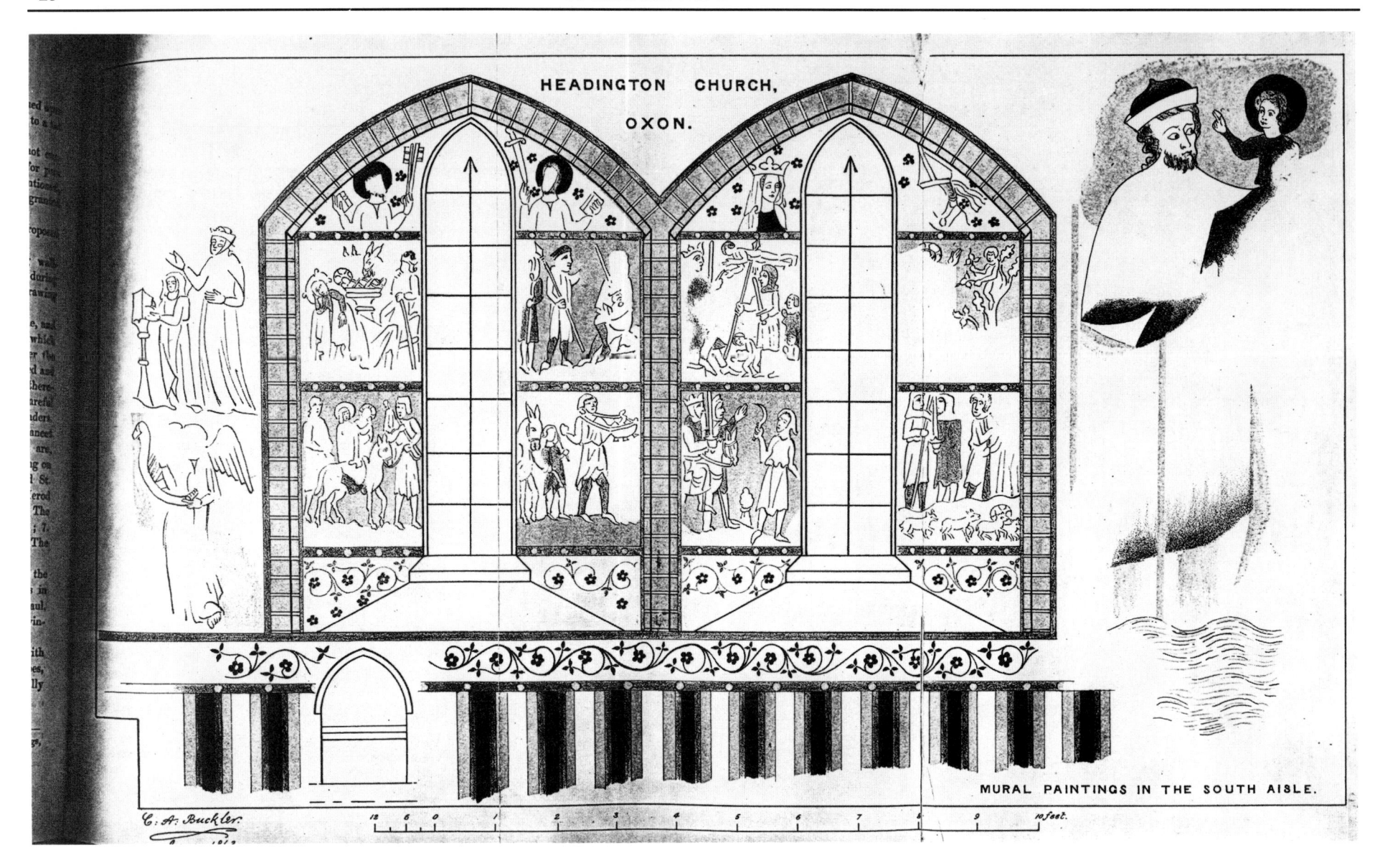

Mural paintings in the south aisle of St. Andrew's Church as recorded by C.A. Buckler in June 1863 taken from Proceedings of the Oxford Architectural and Historical Society *for 1863*

of the chancel and its roof date from this period. The upper stages of the tower seem to have been added in about 1500, possibly under the direction of William Orchard, already referred to in an earlier section. Orchard was a master mason, involved in several building projects in Oxford and elsewhere, who worked one of the largest quarries in the area. The south porch was added in 1598. Part of the tower had to be rebuilt in 1679 and this was recorded not only by Anthony Wood but also by the inscribed initials of the churchwardens of the time on stones on the outside of the tower.

Various repairs were carried out in the eighteenth century, including the rebuilding in part of the east wall and work on the north wall and the roof. A buttress seems to have been erected against the north wall but this was removed in later renovations. The interior of the church was plastered and white-washed, covering the wall-paintings, and the floor was paved. But by 1862 the church was held to be more in need of repair than any church in the diocese and Bishop Wilberforce described it as

> incumbered with galleries and pews, woodwork of different ages and every imaginable shape, position and proportion, the floor well below that of the churchyard, broken and uneven. The roof admits an abundant supply of rain.

Money for restoration was raised by voluntary subscription and the church was extended to the west by J.C. Buckler in 1864, in the lancet style, at a cost of £3,000. Buckler was an architect practising in Oxford, now chiefly known for his drawings of old buildings, and a proponent of careful restoration. His additions at Headington left much of the older work untouched, but it was felt necessary to rebuild the south aisle, which destroyed the thirteenth-century wall-paintings in the Lady Cha-

Box pews in the chancel of St. Andrew's Church (Bodleian Library, MS. Top. Oxon. c. 521)

pel. These were recorded, though, by his son C.A. Buckler, as were other later paintings over the chancel arch and the nave arcading.

A further extension of the church was undertaken in 1881, when the north aisle was added, including a north porch and vestry, at a cost of £2,300. These additions increased the number of seats to 450.

Modern work has included a re-arrangement of the chancel and the creation of a baptistry under the tower in 1961. The ringing-chamber in the tower was restored in 1967 and the six bells were re-hung; two more were added in 1975. The tower was renovated in 1972 and general repairs to the roof and masonry took place between 1977 and 1979, when new lighting, flooring and heating were provided. The roof was painted in what some regard as rather controversial colours and some of the pews were replaced by chairs to provide greater flexibility.

Headington Cross, drawn and engraved by G. Lollis, 1813

For further details of the windows and internal furnishings of the church see:-

St Andrew's Church, Headington, Oxford, a leaflet available in the church

Within Living Memory - Recollections of Old Headington, Oxford, compiled by Leslie and Griselda Taylor published by The Friends of Old Headington

Headington Church north view early in the nineteenth century

The Development of other Churches

By the middle of the nineteenth century the growth of the population, together with the spread of nonconformity, meant that St Andrew's Church could no longer serve all its parishioners, many of whom lived some distance away. In 1848 the church of Holy Trinity in Headington Quarry was founded, the ecclesiastical parish being established in 1850. The church was built of local stone, a gift from Thomas Burrows and dug from Quarry Farm Hollows. Giles Gilbert Scott was the architect and the church cost about £3,000 to build. This sum was raised by voluntary subscription. The building is a simple one, in fourteenth-century style, with nave, north aisle, south porch and a gable bell-cote at the west end. In 1870 the church of All Saints was built in Lime Walk to serve the needs of New Headington. This was replaced in 1910 by the present building in Lime Walk, which is in the Early English style, and has a nave of five bays, north and south aisles and a west porch. The ecclesiastical parish of Highfield was created at the same time as the rebuilding.

Protestant Nonconformity

When Fairfax made Headington his headquarters in 1646 the villagers had ample opportunity to listen to Puritan sermons of high quality. Men came to preach to the General and his army, and many soldiers climbed the trees in the orchard near the General's tent to see and hear. The men of Headington may well have done the same.

Some traces of dissent survived the Restoration. Robert Pawling, who was an Oxford merchant and Mayor in 1679, was the tenant of Magdalen Farm. In 1672 he took out a licence to hold Presbyterian services in a house in Oxford, but he also continued to attend St Andrew's Church. He was involved in a dispute about a pew which traditionally belonged to the farm. He lent the pew to Sir Thomas Whorwood while he was living at Mason's Farm and disputed the right of Sir Thomas's tenant at Manor Farm subsequently to take over the pew. But there seems to have been no real continuity between these seventeenth-century survivals and the nonconformity of the nineteenth century.

Methodism first appeared in Quarry hamlet. As a result of the enclosure dispute the villagers said that

> as they are to be deprived of their funeral path they will not come to church at all but intend to have a Methodist preacher come to them.

This is what happened and meetings began in James Coppock's house. The first chapel was opened in 1830 in Trinity Road; a larger one was built in Quarry High Street in 1860 at a cost of £300, the earlier building being used as a Sunday School until 1874, when a new school building was added on the High Street site. In 1889 a second chapel was opened in Lime Walk at a cost of £300.

From the beginning of the nineteenth century a few families would attend the Baptist Chapel in New Road in Oxford, even though they did not always sever their connections with the parish church. The small mission hall, built in 1836, together with the burial ground in the Croft, was closely associated with the chapel in Oxford. It became independent in 1929.

JULIAN MUNBY *works in Oxford and is an architectural historian.*

Buildings in the village
John Ashdown

This chapter has been written following an examination of some of the historic buildings surviving in Old Headington, assisted by secondary documentary sources. Most of the older buildings are vernacular in character. That is to say they use locally available materials in ways traditionally found satisfactory in terms of layout, appearance and the sound construction of permanent shelter for living and working in. By contrast the parish church and the grand mansions express national supra-vernacular architectural knowledge.

The vernacular building traditions of the Oxford region are notable for their diversity. The wide range of building materials available and the various methods of construction found reflect the complex local geology and the region's position at the centre of southern England, accepting influences from all quarters. Some local villages and towns exhibit a wide range of materials and structural forms in their historic buildings. Other localities, and Old Headington is one, are distinctly homogeneous in character, reflecting a limited local tradition that has only slowly been modified by time and fashion. It is also common enough to find survivals of medieval houses in many Oxfordshire villages. This is not the case in Old Headington where the oldest village buildings illustrate the phenomenon of a great rebuilding in the seventeenth century. Whether the earlier buildings have disappeared as a result of poor construction, neglect or other factors is an open question, but certainly fire damage has to be taken into account in Old Headington.

The buildings to be described are among those now surviving within the limits of the Old Headington Conservation Area. That is the formerly rather isolated nucleated village centre of a large parish occupying an upland position about two miles from the City of Oxford. Until the nineteenth century its main economic activity depended upon agriculture and the stone-quarrying industry. The former placed many of its farms within the village, or nearby, and the latter provided a local source of walling material and construction knowledge. Old Headington's present role as a residential area for Oxford had early beginnings but was increasingly important from the mid-eighteenth century when the development of landscaped parks containing villas for Oxford people began a process that has now removed all obvious traces of the village's historic role. The nineteenth century also saw an increased use of brick walling as the Headington Quarry-Shotover brickworks replaced the earlier stone-quarrying industry on the south-east boundary of the parish. In so far as the historic buildings of Old Headington are concerned it must be restated that the village is located on Lower Corallian rocks, composed of sands and loams with seams of clay, yielding a variable soil. The stone quarries, situated less than a mile to the south-east, exploited Upper Corallian rocks comprising 'raggy' limestones - the rubble-stone Coral Rag, Headington freestones and Headington hard stone, which are much mixed with clays. As a result rubble and ashlar stone are used throughout Old Headington and timber structure is confined to roofs and floors.

The village plan

The historic plan form of the village is a tight nucleated one with accommodation roads leading into the fields. The village, while the focus of the parish, does not lie on a through route to anywhere else. Church Street (St Andrew's Road) and High Street (Old High Street) formed a 7-shaped, almost urban, core to the settlement. The several local routes to Oxford led across the fields, in the general direction of modern Cuckoo Lane, and converged at the top of Headington Hill. It was not until the opening in 1775 of the new route for the Stokenchurch turnpike (London Road) that the present approach roads stabilised. More importantly the creation of landscaped parks for the Manor House and Headington House diverted or closed older routes to Oxford. The sharp-angled bend on Osler Road still remains as a reminder of the forced closure of one of the older direct routes, and makes the village layout more explicit. The grounds of Headington House managed to shrink and half-bury Cuckoo Lane but the diverted route remains open.

Historical Development

While it is certainly difficult to date rubble-stone walls without recognisable features, no building other than the church appears to be earlier than the seventeenth century. Possibly the increased wealth of the seventeenth-century village, as expressed in new permanent stone houses, simply destroyed earlier ones of a less sound quality. Headington as a supplier of agricultural products to the growing city of Oxford, and as a provider of considerable quantities of building stone for college and university expansion, would have been able to share in Oxford's prosperity as the city doubled in size between *c.*1580 and *c.*1680.

Another factor which may have limited the survival of early less well-constructed or any timber-framed houses is fire damage, in what was almost certainly a largely thatched-roofed village. Two fires are recorded in the second decade of the eighteenth century to hint at this possibility. Thomas Hearne, in his diary for 1 May 1718, records as follows:

Yesterday, about four clock in the Afternoon, a Fire began at Heddington near Oxford, wch (the wind being pretty high) in a short time burnt down 24 dwelling Houses besides out Houses, Stacks of Corn, Hay, etc. It began just below the Church, on the right side and then went down the Street that runs Southward, taking all in its way, excepting about two Houses, which were stone buildings, whereas the others were old thatch'd Buildings. Near three Years agoe a Fire happened in the same Street that runs Southward. One Godfrey's House was then burnt. It was now just rebuilt by Contributions he had got. But it is now burnt down again. It began in a Brew-House.

Such destruction was considerable in a small community and one wonders what proportion of the whole was involved.

Some indication of wealth and the number of larger houses in Headington parish in the seventeenth century is offered in the Hearth Tax records of 1665. The parish records 36 taxed houses with a total of 116 hearths. Four houses had 8, 7, 6 and 7 hearths respectively. Nineteen houses had either 4 or 3 hearths, and another nineteen houses had 2 or less. Six householders, all having two hearths, were discharged by poverty.

Walling materials

The ubiquitous historic walling material is stone. This is usually random rubble-stone or coursed rubble freestone with some ashlar freestone. Coursed rubble can vary greatly in quality and with care can produce very regular courses of matching blocks. The jointing, however, is always wide in rubblework. A certain amount of special attention can be seen in some house walls where several courses of random rubble are levelled-up with a regular course. Large freestone blocks were used as quoins to external corners of all sound work and were particularly necessary for random rubble work. In ashlar work the joints can be very fine. These various walling stones are used for houses, farm buildings and outhouses and, most characteristically, for boundary walls.

The use of Headington hardstone was usually limited to building plinths and kerbstones. Coral

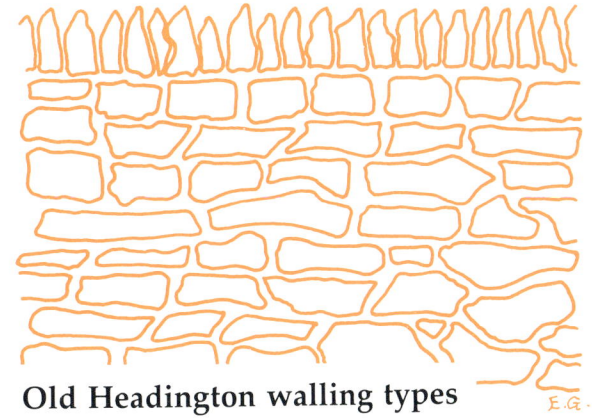

Old Headington walling types
1. Random rubble-stone wall with cock's comb coping

2. Random rubble-stone with quoins

Ragstone made excellent pitched paving. Brick walling becomes common for smaller dwellings, as elsewhere in Oxford, from the 1820s, some with the use of Flemish bond headers. Much of the orange-red brick must come from the Headington Quarry brick-fields on the slopes of Shotover. The brick and tile industry was an expression of Quarry's industrial resilience when the use of Headington stone declined in the early nineteenth century. This was the time when Bath stone became available in Oxford as a result of improved canal and river distribution. However it should be noted that brick was first used in Headington as warm skins to stone walls built for horticultural purposes, at The Rookery garden in 1733 and later for the Headington House garden. Another use of brick in the nineteenth century was for dressings and quoins to rubble-stone work and as a coping top to boundary walls. A limited use of timber weather-boarding exists but is restricted to the gable walls of non-residential buildings.

Lime washing

A further word must be added concerning the external treatment of stone walls of dwelling-houses. In the past they were not left exposed as is now the custom. As in most parts of limestone England, to increase weather protection, house walls were limewashed, often with added natural colours. Most historic stone houses in Old Headington show traces of this practice, with the most common colours being red ochre (red brown) known as ruddle (best seen at 8 The Croft) and yellow ochre (buffs and yellow). Many houses still show traces of alternating brown and yellow coats, some under modern white-paint coatings. A conscious scraping under the demands of late nineteenth- or early twentieth-century taste must account for its universal removal.

Roofing materials

Old Headington lies on the fringe of the normal distribution of natural limestone tiles, and its traditional long-term roof covering is the red clay plain tile of South Oxfordshire. Early photographs, however, suggest that the most common historic roofing material used in the village until the present century was straw thatch. Stonesfield-type stone tiles do, however, survive on a number of roofs. Welsh slate became available once the canal reached Oxford in the 1790s, and increasingly so following the railway links of the 1840s. Welsh slate was used correctly for new buildings with low-pitched roofs, but less successfully visually for the new high-pitched roof of the Mather's Farm barn or for the replacement of thatched roofs on steep pitches. Another nineteenth-century invader, which is only found roofing outbuildings, is the red pantile from Bridgwater in Somerset. The 'double Roman' tiles on the Bell public house outbuildings, as seen from The Croft, are impressed with the head profiles of both Queen Victoria and the Emperor Napoleon III, together with their makers' marks. Replica stone tiles, made from cast concrete, are now to be found on St Andrew's Church and were first introduced to roof the new Black Boy public house in the mid nineteen-thirties. This was one of the first examples of replica stone tiling in the region.

Roofs

Timber is used sparingly for structural purposes in floors and roofs. The seventeenth-century house roofs are held on A-framed trusses with tie and collar, usually two butt-purlins, and the common rafter couples are pegged without a ridge piece. Floor beams and joists where intended to be seen can have simply stopped chamfers.

3. Coursed rubble-stone with quoins

4. Coursed rubble-stone inset with random-rubble

5. Coursed and dressed rubble-stone with quoins and wide joints

BUILDINGS IN THE VILLAGE

It is worthy of note that the roof trusses of some outbuildings (at the White Hart pub, and inside Stoke), and of the barns at Mather's Farm and Bury Knowle are of a characteristic eighteenth/nineteenth-century type. These roofs have trusses with additional inner principle posts between tie and collar under the truss. The Mather's Farm barn (now The Barn, Barton Lane) which has roof trusses of this type is also of particular interest as its roof timbers are of softwood, and some are inscribed with the name GOOD INTENT indicating the ship carrier bringing Baltic timber products to London Docks.

The stone houses of Old Headington

In the absence of inscribed dates on the houses and any access to documents, the chronology adopted here represents received opinion and experience gained elsewhere in Oxford. The earliest domestic buildings belong to the seventeenth century and are represented by a limited variety of house types based on a rectangular plan form. The dominant type has fireplaces and a chimney-stack in each end gable. I find the wide use of the symmetrical end chimney plan a surprise and advanced for such general adoption in the seven-

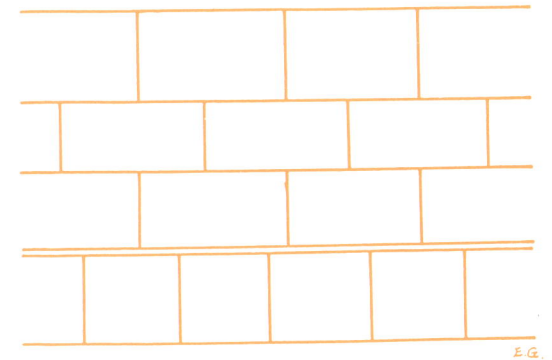

6. Ashlar stone with fine joints and plinth

The Bell PH

teenth century. This factor may be another indication of the special nature of Old Headington, resulting from its close association with the building industry. Equally impressive, however, is the lack of outward show in house design and similarly in structural and joinery details. There is little in these houses that strove to impress the outsider: their basic purpose was to provide sound and comfortable accommodation.

Notably nearly all houses are placed with their long side to the street. The present rear wing of the Bell public house (Old High Street) is, by way of contradiction, set at a right-angle to the street, and has a two-unit plan with side chimney-stacks (not represented elsewhere in Old Headington) and steep-pitched gable roofs of a characteristic seventeenth-century form. Its survival suggests a southern limit for the fire of 1718. Mather's Farmhouse, now much extended, dominates an important location at the centre of the village and still gives an indication of its farming origin, with its barn located to the east and still visually linked

Mather's Farmhouse

to open country. The main house is of three units, with end chimney-stacks expressed externally, all under a stone-tile roof. The rear service wing has a central stack. The main façades have dressed stone mullion windows with cavetto mouldings (hollow quarter round set in square recess). The end chimney plan is, as noted above, an up-to-date one for the seventeenth century and cavetto-moulded windows of this type are found on buildings erected on either side of the Civil War period in Oxford. Mather's Farm is as confident and as prosperous-looking a house as any of its date in Old Headington.

Cavetto-moulded windows only occur elsewhere in Old Headington as a single blocked window in the east wall of the rear wing of Laurel Farm (only visible from the garden of 16 St Andrew's Road). Manor Farm House (Dunstan Road), located west of the village and again uncharacteristically at an angle away from the road, is a large two-storied three-unit seventeenth-century house which is less pretentious than Mather's Farmhouse. It has two

The Conservation Area of Old Headington

Manor Farmhouse

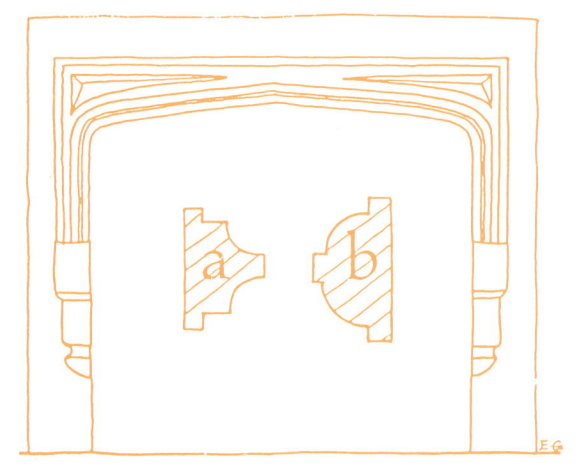

17th century fire place, with sunk spandrils to the arch and the side chamfers stopped.
Inset 17th century window mouldings a. cavetto b. ovolo

flush end chimneys, a steep clay-tiled roof and its windows are of the Oxfordshire vernacular form of three-light wooden casements set in plain openings under exposed oak lintels. The main stone fireplaces are of the typical regional form with sunk spandrils to the arch and the sides chamfer-stopped.

Listed buildings

The following buildings and structures in Old Headington are included on the statutory list of buildings of special architectural or historic interest compiled by the Secretary of State for the Environment. The numbers contained in brackets, when prefaced with 1485 (for Oxford), give a unique reference for a listed building or structure.

BARTON LANE	1	MATHER'S FARMHOUSE (56) with walls to Larkins Lane (56A).
	2	THE BARN (670).
THE CROFT	3	THE COURT (40) with wall to The Croft and Laurel Farm Close (40A).
	4	SANDY LODGE (38) with wall to Osler Road (38A).
	5	CROFT HALL (710) with walls to The Croft (710A).
	6	No 8 (42).
	7	WHITE HART OUTBUILDING (52A).
	8	No 9 (711).
	9	No 11 (41).
	10	No 11A (41).
DUNSTAN ROAD	11	MANOR FARMHOUSE (45) with garden wall (45A).
	12	No 8 (713).
	13	THE ROOKERY - RUSKIN HALL (47) with kitchen garden wall (47A).
LARKINS LANE	14	No 1 (51).
	15	No 2 (51).
	16	No 3 (756).
		THE GRANGE - WALL AND GATE PIERS ONLY (757).
NORTH PLACE	17	No 1 (60).
	18	No 2A (60).
	19	No 2 (60).
	20	BURY KNOWLE HOUSE COACH HOUSE (59).
		BURY KNOWLE PARK WALL (59A).
OLD HIGH STREET	21	No 69 (58).
	22	HEADINGTON HOUSE (37) with walls to The Croft and Cuckoo Lane (37A).
OSLER ROAD	23	WHITE LODGE (38) with wall to Osler Road (38A).
	24	MANOR HOUSE AND STABLE BLOCK (39) with wall to Osler Road (39A).
ST ANDREW'S LANE	25	No 2 (49).
	26	No 4 (49).
	27	No 6 (819).
ST. ANDREWS ROAD	28	CHURCH OF ST. ANDREW (48) with church yard wall (48A).
	29	No 10 (55).
	30	WHITE HART PH No 12 (52) with outbuildings fronting The Croft (52A).
	31	No 14 (46).
	32	No 16 (44).
		pavement in front of Nos 10-14 (821).
STOKE PLACE	33	STOKE (50).

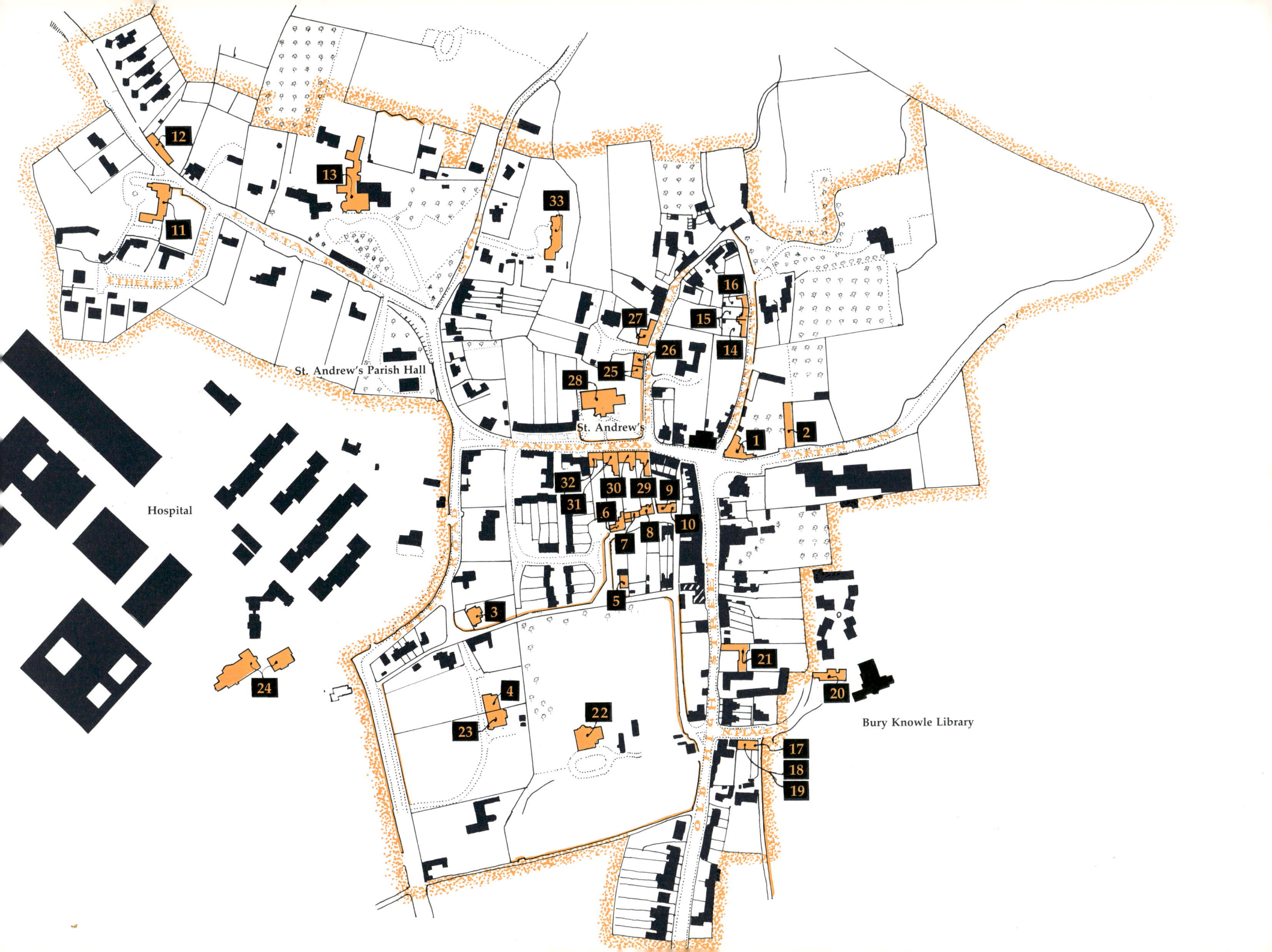

St. Andrew's Parish Hall

Hospital

St. Andrew's

Bury Knowle Library

The Rookery - Ruskin Hall

2 and 4 St. Andrew's Lane

The Court

The Rookery (Ruskin Hall) now hides its seventeenth-century origins within later buildings. One block of John Finch's house of the 1660s remains with a chimney-stack served by two good fireplaces and a number of reset ovolo (bold quarter round) moulded windows survive. Church Hill Farm (4 St Andrew's Lane), where imagination can just reconstruct the farmyard setting, is a two-unit house of two stories with attics built in good coursed rubble with end stacks. It has been extended its full length with an outshot which produces a spectacularly long rear roof, now covered with clay tiles. An important feature of this house is the rear staircase, seen here as a projecting tower. This is a feature which is found in other Old Headington houses and elsewhere in Oxfordshire. The windows at Church Hill Farm are casements under oak lintels. The central entrance has a door-hood unique in Headington, but a common feature of Woodstock, with a single thin stone supported on wrought-iron brackets.

A house now more imposing than its earlier seventeenth-century appearance is The Court (The Croft). It was remodelled about 1924 but preserves a two-unit house with end stacks (and a good fireplace) and has a central entrance opposite a rear-projecting staircase. Its restored leaded cross-casement windows are the only examples of this characteristic but rather polite seventeenth-century type to be seen in Old Headington.

The smaller seventeenth-century houses are less easy to recognize. No.6 St Andrew's Lane (formerly part of the Church Hill Farm complex) and 86 Old High Street are two-unit single-storey houses (with attics) with a single end chimney-stack. No.86 has a very impressive fireplace, suggesting a special function, but is now externally as unpretentious as any of the older houses in the village. This house must also have withstood the fire damage of 1718.

No 6 St. Andrews Lane

10-16 St. Andrew's Road

No one who stands atop the tower of St Andrew's Church can fail to be impressed by the tight, almost urban, character of the village streets seen from above. This feeling of urbanity and sense of place would have been even more apparent before the row of houses west of the church and the old Black Boy public house were demolished, and the new building lines set back. The devastation of the fire of 1718 can also be judged from the tower top. It is unlikely to have come any further west than the present 8 St Andrew's Road. The four two-storied (with attics) houses (10, 12, 14 and 16 St Andrew's Road), all placed longways along the street right at the back of the pavement and opposite the church, are an impressive group. Collectively they belong to the late seventeenth and early eighteenth centuries and are stopped on the west by the early nineteenth-century Laurel Farm house which is set back a little. Except for the more humble No.16 these houses are built of coursed rubble of varying competence and are all covered with red clay tiles. No.16 is built of random rubble, now painted, and is two-storied with attics over a two-unit plan with end stacks. At some stage it functioned as a pair of cottages, each with a winder staircase. The leaded iron casements under oak lintels to the first-floor front windows are a precious survival. Nos.12 and 14 St Andrew's Road are also late seventeenth-century houses but there the similarity ends. Church House (No.14) has been much modified in the 1880s and 1930s and now presents a neo-Georgian elegance through the rubble stone, with sash windows and a classical door case. The location of its earlier windows can still be made out. In plan No.14 is a two-unit house with end stacks.

The White Hart public house (No.12) represents a use of long standing, and occupies a very long property with a front wall of two builds. Its plan, however, fits comfortably about a central chimney-stack in line with a rear projecting staircase. The use of the central chimney-stack here and at No.10 next door is noteworthy and rather archaic in the context of the overwhelming number of more flexibly planned end-chimney houses in Old Headington. The windows of the White Hart retain wooden casements under exposed oak lintels.

The finest house of this impressive row is No.10 St Andrew's Road, which has been described as a refronted seventeenth-century house. It could also be a new house built in the decade either side of 1700. The puzzle is the bold two-unit plan, with a small room each side of a central chimney-stack. The entrance is placed by the extreme west side wall and not in line with the central rear projecting stair tower built in stone. The front wall is carefully built in squared blocks of random course size and the elevation is finished with a coved cornice moulding. There is a contemporary service wing behind the house, later extended. The oak dog-

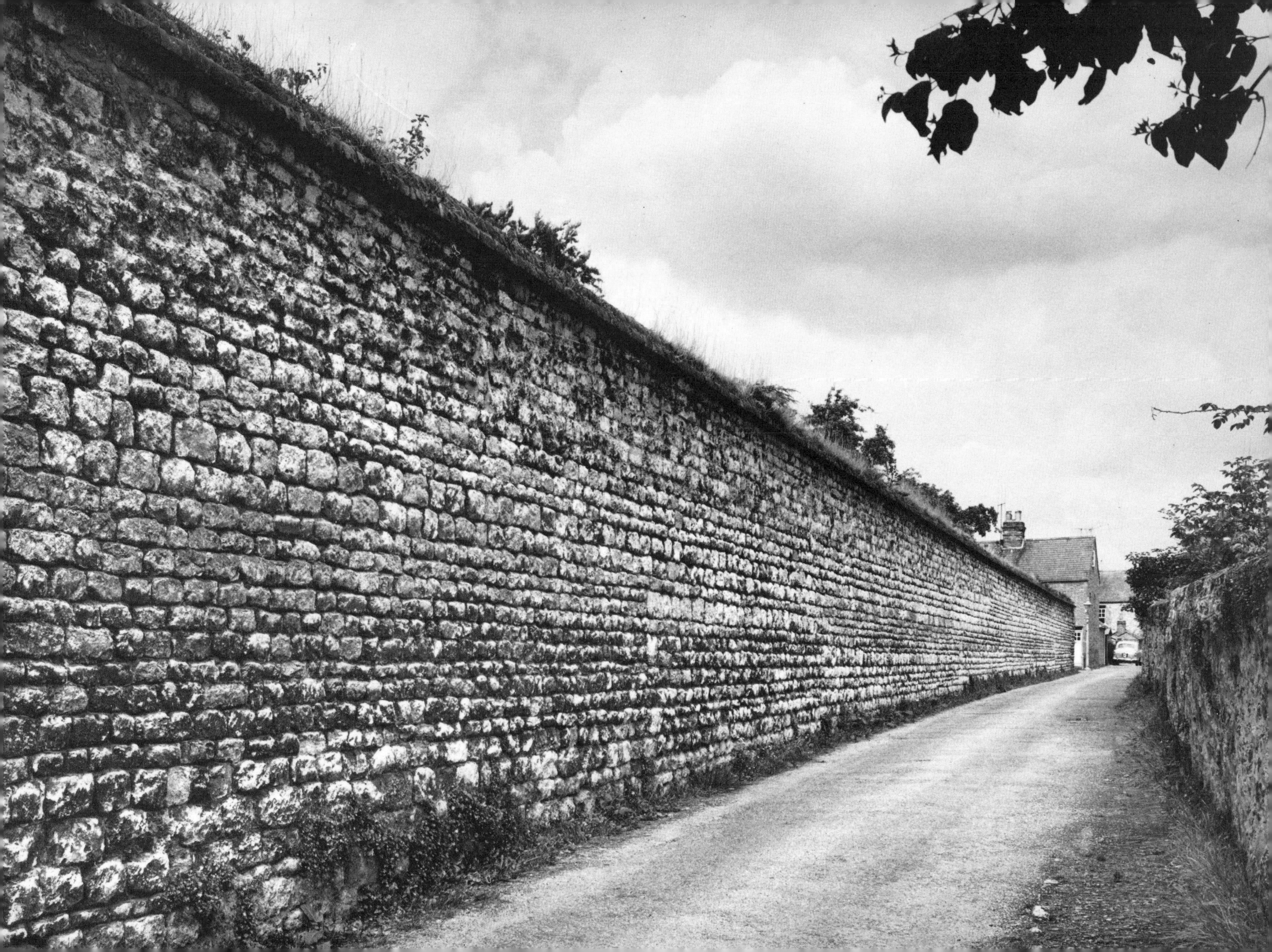

legged staircase, one of the best of its date in Oxford, is outstanding in Old Headington and has good turned balusters; it serves from ground to attics. The refined sash-windows to the front elevation are late eighteenth-century or early nineteenth-century replacements. The two smaller casement windows at the front and the two pairs at the rear are precious early eighteenth-century survivals with thick sash-like glazing bars and inward opening casements. The possible alternative solution to all these features is that a seventeenth-century central chimney lobby-entry house was damaged in the 1718 fire and reconstructed soon afterwards.

An important aspect of 10-16 St Andrew's Road (and possibly other lost houses to the east) was the ownership of land running to the south, some of which is now absorbed by the Headington House grounds, and what remains is cut by branches of The Croft. This back lane made it possible to erect service outbuildings to the St Andrew's Road houses, with independent access. Only those at the White Hart remain as such, with interesting trussed roofs, some with inner principles, covered with stone tiles and representing a precious survival of the vernacular. Nos. 9, 11 and 11A The Croft, which now look very attractive as single-storey cottages (with attics), are conversions in the eighteenth or nineteenth centuries of similar service buildings. No.11 has window lintels with keystones. No.8 The Croft, while occupying a similar service position to 14 St Andrew's Road, was erected as a dwelling house with the given date of 1706. This two-storey house with attics, constructed of rubble stone, is of two units between end stacks with a central entrance and winder stair and a rear service wing. The house is noteworthy for its traces of red ruddle-lime wash, the use of ashlar for a projecting first-floor band course and for the lintels to the window heads which have projecting keystones, clearly indicating an eighteenth-century date. The decent timber casement windows, while renewed, greatly enhance its appearance.

Staircase at 10 St. Andrew's Road

9 - 11 The Croft

No 8 The Croft

Another well-preserved small early eighteenth-century house is No.2 Larkins Lane, where the Headington ashlar also exhibits the use of keystones to window heads, where decent casements remain. The use of ashlar at the vernacular level does not mean that the use of rubble declined, but may indicate the increased local availability of the Headington freestone due to its declining use in Oxford for better quality buildings.

Several smaller houses built in rubble, with oak lintels to windows, should belong to the first half of the eighteenth century and include No.1 Larkins Lane, Nos.1 (a type of lobby entry house) and 2 North Place (which are not contemporary), No.1 Stoke Place, 43 and 45 Old High Street, and 74 Old High Street. Another small coursed-rubble stone house, originally single-storied, survives at No.3 Larkins Lane and carries an additional storey faced in brick over a century later, all now disguised by paint. The ground floor retains sideways sliding sashes. A similar evolution can be seen at 39/41 Old High Street. No 79, Old High Street has a well-preserved eighteenth-century ashlar front with a hardstone plinth to a single-storey house. Its attic is lit with the traditional Headington dormer and the fixed ground-floor window has thick eighteenth-century glazing bars.

Lower Farm (8 Dunstan Road), a plain late eighteenth- or early nineteenth-century house of coursed rubble with a three-unit plan and flush end stacks under a slate roof, can mark the turn into the nineteenth century. It has modified sash-windows under oak lintels, but the use of double-hung sashes looks original. While fully a local building Lower Farmhouse, with its mix of vernacular and polite sources, heralds the end of the true vernacular traditions and the emergence of overriding national fashions. The front range of Laurel Farmhouse (20 St Andrew's Road) shows

1 - 3 Larkins Lane

1, 2 and 2A North Place

No 8 Dunstan Road

that process completed. This is a text-book example of the third decade of the nineteenth century with refined double-hung sash-windows, set in a ruled stucco façade under a low-pitched Welsh slate roof. The front door has a fanlight which echoes Oxford's Beaumont Street. Unity House (8 St Andrew's Lane) is a simpler house of a similar date. Naturally enough while the quarries remained productive, houses continued to be built in stone well into the nineteenth century. Dwellings such as 83 Old High Street, with margin lights to

Headington House

The Manor House

its sash-windows, and the adjoining No.81 show the trends. What might be described as the North Oxford influence is not conspicuous, except at St Andrew's House (St Andrew's Road) built for the wine merchant John Mason in 1862. This rather gaunt gothic house in coursed rubble looks every inch the Vicarage it was to become until the 1970s. Much less committed to gothic are stone buildings like 10 St Andrew's Lane, with its minimum of conscious detail. The later private side of the house is faced in buff brick of quite a different character. Another prominently sited rubble stone building is Linden House (The Priory, Old High Street). Here we know the name of the architect, employed by Major-General Desborough to reconstruct the house before 1884. This was H.G.W. Drinkwater of Oxford who designed here in a 'sweetness and light' Queen Anne style and dressed the rubble-stone with red brick to good effect. As Desborough was the first chairman of the British Workman (65 Old High Street), now Viking Sports Club, it is likely that Drinkwater designed those premises in 1880 in a more picturesque Old English half-timbered style over a rubble-stone base. The same mix of materials is found at 87 and 89 Old High Street, a semi-detached pair of half-timbered houses, built by the local builder Charlie Morris which are helpfully inscribed 1909. They are also labelled Linden-Cottages on their 'Jacobean' dragon brackets. Noticeably the rubble-stone used is an imported brown rubble, confirming that the local supply was gone.

The Mansions and Villas

A distinct class of large dwelling houses, standing in their own parkland, was attracted to Old Headington in the second half of the eighteenth century. The earliest, a sober Georgian design fronted in ashlar stone discreetly sited close to the village, was Headington House. This was built in 1775-1783 for William Jackson, the Oxford printer. This was followed by the Manor House, completed before 1779 for Sir Banks Jenkinson, sixth Baron Walcot, in ashlar to a late Palladian villa model.

White Lodge

Sandy Lodge

1 and 2 St. Andrew's Road

Joseph Lock, the Oxford goldsmith and banker, erected Bury Knowle, probably before 1804, as a neo-classical villa with very refined Headington ashlar. The earlier house at The Rookery (Ruskin Hall) was refronted with a plain mansion block in 1810. Headington Lodge, said to have been built about 1835 and since 1922 divided and extended as White Lodge (Osler Road) and Sandy Lodge (The Croft), represents the 'Regency' villa. It is faced with painted stucco and has good canopy iron-work. The Grange (formerly Elmbank, Larkins Lane), had, by the middle of the nineteenth century, completed the encirclement of the village by mansions in parks. A remarkable fact is that we do not know the name of a single architect of one of these houses.

The brick houses of Old Headington

We must now return to the early nineteenth century to record the introduction of brick work in the construction of the smaller houses. This was usually associated with lower pitched roofs carrying Welsh slate. Two brick traditions are present, the use of local orange-coloured Headington Quarry-Shotover reds and the Midland English formula of diaper-header face-work in Flemish bond.

The most prominent early nineteenth-century use of red brick is in the three-storied pair of houses Nos.1 and 3 St Andrew's Road. These double-fronted houses have sash windows (casements in the attic) and stone dressings to quoins and openings, under a Welsh slate roof. They make a telling local contrast to the contemporary Laurel Farm or Oxford's Beaumont Street. Even so they must have made a considerable impact when new, in terms of colour and as an advertisement for the new local brick industry. No.101 Osler Road, a lodge to the Manor House estate, shows the same new spirit in a small house of pretensions, with fine rubbed-brick segmental arches to the window heads.

Many of the smaller terraced houses built in Old Headington between 1825 and 1850 reflected the building practices then current in Oxford's inner suburbs of St Ebbe's and Jericho. This included the use of grey header bricks to produce attractive Flemish bond façades, set with fully divided sash-windows. These can be seen, for example, at Nos.2-5 The Croft and 37 St Andrew's Road. One precious survival is the small detached Shotover red brick house, now containing a domestic garage, at 58 Old High Street. The use of timber lintels and casements suggests this, and probably also 51 Old High Street - also in Shotover reds with

No 69 Old High Street

Mather's Barn

Croft Hall

headers - to be the work of local Headington tradesmen.

The builders' houses of the later nineteenth century are also generally paired or terraced, but are built without Flemish bond work. The Shotover bricks are contrasted with courses of buff ones and with Bath stone dressings and lintels. A careful look also shows that brick-faced houses often have walls of stone to side and rear elevations, indicating that the use of brick was expensive and a matter of fashionable demand. Only one group of these later brick-faced houses has a date plaque. This is at 3 Stoke Place which reads 'Rookery Cottages 1885'. However, the 1876 Ordance Survey Map shows that most of these brick houses were built after the survey was carried out.

Some other buildings of Old Headington

It was characteristic of a nineteenth-century village still to contain work places. Two surviving buildings, now disguised, reflect this. The brick-built bakery complex in St Andrew's Lane, next to 'The Old Stables' development, is relevant if undistinguished architecturally. The Malthouse complex formerly existing between Old High Street and Bury Knowle has left fewer traces. This was sold and broken up in 1880 and in part provided a site for the British Workman (now Viking Sports Club) with its barn becoming part of Bury Knowle. The Malthouse itself was demolished, leaving a long wing at right angles to the road as a dwelling house, now 69 Old High Street (The Hermitage).

Between 1912 and 1925 C.F. Bell, Keeper of Fine Art at the Ashmolean Museum, carried out a remarkably tasteful conversion in such a way that the wing now appears to be a convincing early eighteenth-century house. One private school building of the early twentieth century at 41a St Andrew's Road deserves a mention for its acquired primitive charm. The old tin hut of Miss Steff's dame school is a relic of a once common transportable 'off-the-peg' industrial building system, with its painted corrugated iron cladding.

The twentieth century

C.F. Bell's careful academic house conversion was not alone. An equally sophisticated enhancement was carried out by 1924 (date on door-hood) at The Court (The Croft) by Lord Sholto Douglas. Sir Charles Nicholson the architect settled at 14 St Andrew's Road and embellished by 1933 (date on bay to garden) the house already extended by H.J. Tollit for Mrs Edgecombe before 1884. In 1932 Stanley Hamp of Collcut and Hamp enlarged the Manor Farmhouse for R.W. Rose-Innes in a picturesque modernist rubble-stone style typical of its time.

Stanley Hamp had come to Headington in 1931 with a very different conception of architectural truth in mind. He had been commissioned by the Radcliffe Infirmary Trustees to build a house for their administrator, A.G.E. Sanctuary. Manor House Corner (59 Osler Road, now William Osler House), when finished was considered significant enough to be illustrated in the *Architectural Review*

The Manor House Stable block

in 1934 and is the only house in the Oxford area built in the white-rendered square modern style of the 1930s.

Recent development has on the whole been kind to Old Headington. The growth of a twentieth-century suburb constrained by its older village buildings and walls can, however, never be an easy one. Until recently the concrete-block houses Nos. 10-18 Dunstan Road designed by Ahrends, Burton and Koralek (1967-8) were the most frankly extrovert group of new dwellings, found acceptable here presumably because of their fringe location. The local authority housing within Bury Knowle Park, under construction 1986-7 in contrasting bricks, must mark another extreme but should provide a most attractive environment. Though big and modern Emden House (1981 by Philip Del Nevo) is saved by its traditional outer skin from upsetting a more public setting. Consciously seeking to keep the balance is the local authority Laurel Farm development (1985-6). Two recent successful pieces of positive conservation have been the conversion of the Mather's Farm Barn and the early nineteenth-century Baptist Chapel (known as Croft Hall) to dwelling houses.

The most dramatic modern change results from the social and visual dominance of the John Radcliffe Hospital, sited within the Manor House grounds. As a result Old Headington illustrates very clearly the contrasts of late twentieth-century England where our preservation of historic buildings must rely on an illusion transcending space and time. When the conserved character and *genius loci* combine, as in much of Old Headington, we are seeing the best balance of the past and present that we can hope for in our time.

Grateful acknowledgements and thanks are made to all those house-owners who granted access and discussed their houses with me. Special acknowledgement is also made to the contributors and compilers of *Within Living Memory*.

JOHN ASHDOWN *is the Conservation Officer for Oxford City Council.*

Development and the protection of character
Roger France

Before its absorption into the city in 1929, the village of Headington had connections with Oxford through its wealthier and more learned residents who commuted into the city. One of the results has been the subdivision of larger tracts of land for development and the refurbishment of older houses. In the tradition of much new building in collegiate Oxford, proposals for change have often been accompanied by hearty argument, and in Old Headington similar proposals have assumed a character of their own. In this chapter we shall look at some of the key developments that have taken place in the twentieth century, and then consider them in the light of our understanding of village character and its preservation in the face of change.

St. Andrew's Road

The first example of historic preservation took place between the wars. Where 27-33 St. Andrew's Road now stands there had been a group of seventeenth-century cottages built up to the highway. In the 1930s there were moves at national level to encourage the improvement of older housing (see also p.55), and the National Federation of Housing Societies had taken a lead in promoting such rehabilitation. In 1936 it was learned that Oxford City Council were preparing an order for the demolition of these cottages. Under the leadership of Alic Smith, Warden of New College, ten local residents joined together to purchase the cottages so that these could be rehabilitated. Fielding Dodd was appointed architect and a scheme of renovation drawn up and approved by the Council; his proposals show much opening up of the interiors of the cottages, some new additions at the rear and complete refenestration.

At the outset Dodd had expressed doubts about the practicality of rehabilitation; when building

Plan of Old Headington between the wars showing cottages aligned up to the public highway

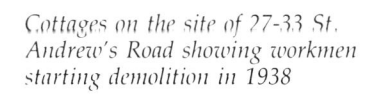

Cottages on the site of 27-33 St. Andrew's Road showing workmen starting demolition in 1938

When built, the terrace of cottages in St. Andrew's Road was set back from the public highway and it had to lose its thatch

Fielding Dodd's proposals for a redeveloped terrace on the site of the old cottages; it shows a curved frontage to follow the road alignment and a thatched roof

work was under way the structural condition of the cottages was found to be too bad for economical repair, so a scheme of redevelopment was drawn up and approved by the Council. This new terrace has several features of design interest as an early exercise in urban conservation. First, Dodd attempted to remain in sympathy with the alignment of the road; the setback of the houses was probably due to the council's insistence on building lines. Secondly, he kept to thatch for the roof, thus softening an elevation that would otherwise be harsh. Here he ran into difficulties: because of confusion between the Ministry of Health and the Local Authority over the waiving of byelaws for thatch he had to resort to using tiles. Thirdly, he kept the materials and details sympathetic to the tradition of the village. Looking at the terrace today, Dodd's design could benefit from softening: in some senses it is similar to Lutyens' earlier cottage terrace at Ashby St. Ledgers (1908), but without its grandeur. In spite of these shortcomings, though, we are left with an early and innovative exercise in sympathetic redevelopment.

William Orchard Close

After the second world war a development of interest took place in William Orchard Close. In 1959 a firm of speculative developers, Span, bought the field to the north of the churchyard from the executor of Mr Robert Wylie. A meeting of residents was held to discuss the proposed plans and the result of this meeting was the creation of The Friends of Headington. The Friends were successful in influencing the Council's negotiations with the developers who had put forward several proposals before the Council refused the application. The developers appealed to the Minister of Housing and Local Government, but lost. They then sold the site to a group of Friends who had by this time formed a consortium for its purchase. (See also p.61)

William Orchard Close showing modest, clean-cut houses in the post-Festival of Britain mode. Although the tint of the brickwork matches the local stone, there is no attempt to echo architectural shapes or detailing

The site for development to the north of St. Andrew's Church showing the scheme drawn up by Gerald Banks in 1963 with its dispersed arrangement of detached houses

One of the objections put forward by the Friends was that the Span proposals had windows that were too large and that this would permit a lack of privacy; in common with other Span developments, there was also a high density of dwellings on the site. After the announcement of the appeal decision, a local architect, Gerald Banks, was approached and a much looser site plan produced. Here, we see a plain, tarmacadam approach with larger houses grouped informally around this space. The main space is visually sewn together by garden walls of indigenous height; the architecture is modest and clean with low-pitched roofs characteristic of many new buildings in the fashion of the 1950s. These houses are not slavish copies of the past, in terms of architectural scale the design of William Orchard Close can certainly be said to be sympathetic with its neighbours in the village. On the other hand, some of the details - painted bargeboards, for example - appear uncomfortably dominant and the roadscape stark. Although the houses are closely gathered, there are disconcerting gaps at the corners where the relationship between individual buildings and the group has not been resolved. (See also p.61)

Dunstan Road

A startling change occurred when development was proposed at the western approach to the village in Dunstan Road. An application for a scheme of housing had been received by the City Council to develop this slender slice of land with its dramatic northwards views. The plans were opposed by the Friends, and in the process of discussions a group of prospective owners came forward and commissioned Ahrends, Burton and Koralek to produce a design. This firm of architects had only recently been formed, although its partners were already well known in Oxford for their work on the design of the new Oxford Centre

The north-western extremity of Old Headington village showing 10-18 Dunstan Road, designed by Ahrends, Burton and Koralek in 1974 for a group of prospective owners. A few simple component shapes are threaded together, given unity by a dominant material and then softened by planting

for Management Studies at Kennington. The problem that faced the architects was to design the impossible: five houses for a joint client which combined the conflicting requirements of southwards sun, northwards view, and privacy. They succeeded with a highly articulated plan that is low in profile, small in scale and recessive in tone. Here we see a different approach to architectural style and the setting. The houses are part of each other, and do not display the individualism that is evident in William Orchard Close; yet the development as a whole has distinction, due to the visual interest in the shape of the elevation, and to the rich textures of garden wall, front access space and blockwork elevations. The combination of a single elevational material with a few simple shapes that are repeated, articulated and softened with planting produces an architecture of sympathy and panache.

Laurel Farm

Only late in the story of Old Headington has the local authority played its part in the development of the village. The building of Laurel Farm Close is the result of the contribution made by Oxford City Council. Initially, though, it was the Friends of Old Headington who sought to find an acceptable solution for the development of the land originally belonging to the farm and which had for some years been in the ownership of Corpus Christi College. They had worked with the College to find an acceptable layout for housing, and on this basis the College sold the site to the Council in 1976 with outline planning permission for seventeen dwellings. In 1983 the Council produced proposals for twenty-two dwellings with integral car parking facilities. These proposals showed a system of segregated pedestrian and vehicular access with a pedestrian alley on the east of the site and a cul-de-sac road on the west.

Being both developer and planning authority, the City Council has to consult central government for approval as well as undertake normal local consultations. As they had owned the site since 1976, these stages were undertaken with notable haste: the scheme was completed in 1986 - although without the garages. The simple design theme is evident. The contrast between the tightness of the

Laurel Farm, designed by the City Council Architects' Department in 1983. The architectural style is consciously neo-vernacular. The grouping of houses along the pedestrian way is tight and impressive and the whole vista unified by the skilful paving. An attempt to return to the lighter village scene

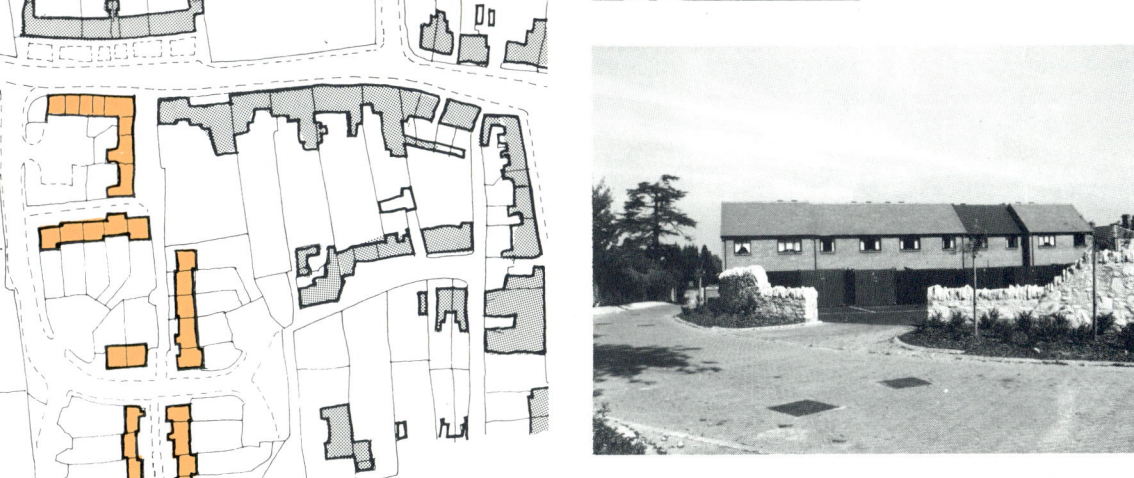

The rear view of houses at Laurel Farm is less satisfactory, especially the over-simple roof, the inexplicable change in roof tile and the indeterminate end

main footway and the open spaces across the gardens properly reflect the scale and character of the traditional village, although the architecture is as much urban as it is rural. But the cranking of the vehicular access road seems pointless and much of the architectural detailing looks contrived. One reason for this may be the use of red brick, a material not much used in Old Headington until the nineteenth century. Concrete, stone and thatch are much bolder and simpler materials and intricate detailing in these materials is more difficult; in these respects, the scheme is more urban than rural. In spite of this, the Council's scheme must rank as a sensitive innovation in the evolution of municipal housing in the city.

The Buchanan Study

Over the post-war years it had become evident to residents that the continuing development of land, increasingly heavy traffic flows and changes in household occupancy were continuing to alter the character of the village. Old Headington, it seemed, was undergoing an incremental transformation that was barely understood and unquantified. Accordingly, the Friends appointed Colin Buchanan and Partners to undertake a survey of the village. The report was published in 1976 and advised on:

(i) the amount of new development that should be allowed within the Conservation Area;
(ii) solutions to the increasing problem of through traffic;
(iii) design guidelines and building form;
(iv) the boundary of the Green Belt.

In making their recommendations the authors of the report were basing their ideas upon the notion of capacity: that to retain its character the village would have to establish limits to the amount and type of housing provision, and to the quantity of

Type of Housing	Number of Dwellings	Density (Dw./Acre)	% total dwellings	% total development area
1. Urban	69	10	43.5	20.5
2. Rural	27	14	17.0	6.0
3. Detached	29	2.1	18.0	40.0
4. Housing Closes	31	8.6	19.5	10.5
5. Houses in large Private Grounds	3	0.4	2.0	23.0
TOTALS	**159**	**4.5 (av)**	**100%**	**100%**

Source: Buchanan and Partners, Old Headington: Final Report *(1976)*

self-generated traffic and through traffic. Densities and intensities were seen to be crucial elements in this assessment. In their conclusion, the authors presented guidelines to assist in the control of development; they recommended the tightening of the village boundary, and the infilling of land within that boundary

> only at densities and in building forms that are compatible with the existing environment.

The authors undertook a detailed analysis of the types of housing in the village. Nearly half of all houses (44%) were urban in character: this was defined as being mainly terraced, facing main roads and of mixed social occupancy. Much of the balance was made up of rural (17%), detached (18%) or close development (19%). Rural housing was mainly terraced development fronting main roads; detached housing was standing in its own ground with high car ownership, and closes were defined as special groupings around paved courts shared by vehicles and pedestrians. It can be seen that the housing which gives the strongest visual image - urban and rural - accounts for the largest proportion of housing (60.5%), although this

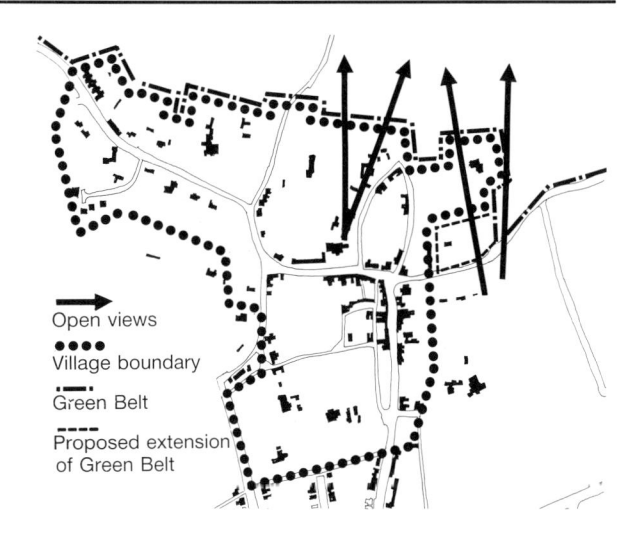

Simplified version of one of the analytical maps by Colin Buchanan and Partners showing their proposals for an extension to the Green Belt and a tightly drawn village boundary

occupies only a quarter of the total area. It is this core of buildings which also contains the oldest buildings.

The authors also looked at the problem of traffic. Generally, they concluded that the village was approaching the limits of its ability to act as a short-cut for through traffic and also for self-generated traffic. Usefully, the authors combined these two concepts, advising that:

> ...if nothing can be done about the 'through' traffic element... to allow additional development will merely exacerbate an already unsatisfactory situation... On the other hand, if the 'through' traffic can be diverted, then a limited amount of new development could be tolerated.

They recommended that if the three sites under consideration at that time (Laurel Farm Close,

Emden House and Bury Knowle) were developed

> within the next year or two; this would set an undesirably fast pace of growth.

In the decade following the publication of this recommendation, these three new estate developments have been built, adding

> ...people to the residential population and ...cars.

One further aspect of preservation was proposed by the authors: the extension of the Green Belt so that the connection between the countryside and the village could be retained. Along Barton Road, they proposed the extension of the green belt up to Mather's Farm barn. This would enable the important visual link from the 'Black Boy' junction to be retained, and allow the rural setting of the surrounding countryside to penetrate unbroken to London Road, on its way passing through the eighteenth-century landscape of Bury Knowle Park. Here, in the Buchanan report, we find elucidation of two important issues, housing and traffic, and the first steps in positive planning by the presentation of a set of proposals for guiding change.

1976 to 1986

In the ten years following the Buchanan report much building took place. The Council's development at Laurel Farm brought 23 new houses. Emden House produced 26 new flats and Bury Knowle heralded a further 29 dwellings. So Buchanan's figure of 159 dwellings is increased to 237, a rise of 49%. In a discussion of conservation policy, we have to ask how many more dwellings might be expected in the forseeable future, and at what point these expansions impinge upon policies for the preservation of character. Indeed, might not such a position have already been reached?

Recent Council sheltered housing at the back of Bury Knowle library

Two planning applications generated much discussion at the end of this period. The first was an application for two 'executive' houses as speculative developments in St. Andrew's Lane. The initial designs were extensively modified following advice from the Friends and their Planning Consultant. The Council was unable to find grounds to refuse this application. The second was submitted by the Architects' Design Partnership for the construction of a single dwellinghouse on a small plot of land in The Croft at the heart of the village. On one side are houses, and on the other a converted chapel, which is a freestanding structure with The Croft footpath on three sides. The council refused this application, partly for reasons of visual amenity and partly because of difficulty of access. On appeal, the inspector supported the local authority, and in the letter of decision it was noted that

> the unbuilt areas of open space...make an important contribution to the character and appearance of the Conservation Area... and accentuate and enhance its special quality.

It is precisely this argument that had been adopted by the Friends in their representations, namely, that the spaces in a village are as important as the buildings in the definition of village character.

The Role of Local Authorities

It is the function of the Local Authority to control changes to the built environment, and this it achieves through the Town and Country Planning Acts. Over the years, this branch of legislation has reflected the move towards the retention and renewal of the inherited built fabric. In doing this, the landscape of settlements has been enriched with continuity of the past, smallness of scale and topographical uniqueness, qualities often absent in the larger mass building of the nineteenth and twentieth centuries. Protecting this heritage is achieved in two ways. The first is through the compilation of a list of buildings of special architectural and historic interest - "listed buildings". The character of these buildings is protected by law, and the permission of the local planning authority is needed before any change - interior or exterior - is made. The second method of protection is by the declaration of a Conservation Area. Any work of demolition inside such an area needs 'conservation consent' from the local planning authority. (Listed buildings and the boundary of the Conservation Area are shown in figure 37). The process of protection needs the fullest possible statement of character so that judgements can be made about changes that might be allowed. But the essence of the legislation is to preserve; changes can be additions or replacements, but it is in the detail of a conservation policy that its effectiveness will lie.

In its Local Plan for Oxford, the City Council says:

> the quality of a place...depends very much upon the relationship between its buildings, their shape, size and details of wall materials, the design of spaces between them, and of individual objects... (Para 9.37)

> Conservation Areas...contain important buildings...The spaces and the 'furniture', trees and pavings are also important in contributing to the character and context of the area. (Para 9.42)

Both the City Council and the County Council have statements of policy which give general support to the preservation of architectural and historic character. Indeed, the City Council saw little problem in 1973 when it issued its publicity pamphlet on the Conservation Area. It said that it was the policy of the council to:

> ensure retention, where this is still possible, of the individual character of the many suburbs. Although there is no specific threat to the character of Old Headington, a continuous natural process of change must be expected to occur....

It is with these statements of intent that the local authority sets out to preserve and enhance the architectural and historic character of Old Headington and other Conservation Areas in Oxford.

A brief look at these sites in Old Headington gives us a valuable sample of styles of development in terms of their appearance and instigation. And central to their development has been the influence of the local community. Although each site has been designed in a different architectural style, each has paid respect to the neighbourhood in its own particular way. These examples raise important issues with respect to the preservation of history, architectural compatibility, and the character of the village.

Preservation and the future

Having looked at these twentieth-century developments, one important question emerges: to what extent should the notion of historic preservation prevent the natural process of evolution and the normal progress of property capitalization? In each example, designers have sought to make their buildings compatible in terms of colour, scale and materials. The owners of the sites have not questioned their own right to make additions to the urban scene. The common good has been represented by the observations of the Friends, by the decisions of the local authority and by the Secretary of State. Architectural style is normally the province of the architect, and the relationship of the building with respect to its setting is the province of the town planner. In an age when there is no common grammar with respect to architectural style, instinct can be as important as logic in the design of buildings. In this context the appearance of every building is the product of the individualism of the designer and the rules of community acceptability.

In the early days of the Town and Country Acts local planning authorities placed strong emphasis on the zoning of land and on the density of its use. Over the years, helped by increasing local authority discretion and greater public participation, this simple clarity has been lost. As far as the village of Old Headington is concerned, the Council's latest policy statement and its powers of discretion and interpretation are the only guards against all manner of growth. There is no doubt that tighter controls should exist. Indeed, looking at the quantity and rate of development in the decade following the Buchanan study, it could be argued that such a move is overdue. A preservation policy has to start with a clear understanding of what preservation means, and how this relates to individual buildings and composite groups. In doing this, it distinguishes between changes that reinforce historic character and changes that dilute. And this should lead to guidelines for the acceptability of further building and its location. In identifying this the Friends have again demonstrated innovation: herein lies the hope that in the year 2087 the historic character of Old Headington will still be largely intact and enjoyed by our successors.

ROGER FRANCE *is an architect and town planner and is tutor in urban conservation at Oxford Polytechnic.*

An artist's idea of 'the windmill' (Bodleian Library, Minn Coll. Neg. 105/8...) from an original drawing in the collections of Corpus Christi College)

The present century

Leslie Taylor

Oxford has always been fringed by hamlets and villages but in the early years of the century several of these districts were setting up their own Councils and later they were to become part of the City Authority. Such were Iffley, Wolvercote, Quarry, Barton and Old Headington. But they all retained their individual characteristics which were recognised by the City.

It is this individuality which is one of their main attractions and which many of us who are fortunate enough to live in them are anxious to preserve. So let us take a closer look at this attractiveness, which is reflected in the scarcity of properties available for sale, and their prices, especially in Old Headington. Certainly there is a charming mix of pleasant dwellings in a unique setting. And there are those folk who once lived here and those who still do many of whom would agree that it is not merely an agreeable place in which to live but a way of life. I think perhaps that some of the ways in which the village has developed may fill in a few answers to the question of what draws people to Old Headington; I will reminisce and see what emerges.

When I returned to Oxford in 1940 I remember feeling strongly that Old Headington was the place where I was keen to live. I looked around but without success, so I had to be content with Iffley Turn. But good fortune came my way in 1944 when my wife and I were able to rent a house in a small crescent of four houses in Church Street, renamed St Andrew's Road in 1955. These cottages - they were always known as cottages - had been built to replace ten old thatched cottages which were condemned in the late 1930s (see also p.48). Some local residents - including Dr John Johnson, Printer to the University, Professor E.G.T. Liddell of The Hermitage, Dr A.B. Emden, Principal of St

The footpath still leading to Mr. Talboys' old cottage

Stone walls, green verges, cobble kerbs and open views are just a few features of the village

Edmund Hall, and Alic Smith, Warden of New College - had put up the money to build the crescent with the aim of showing how careful design and building might preserve the old character. The four new houses to replace the ten thatched cottages were handed over in 1939 to the Oxford Preservation Trust who sold them on long lease (999 years) at a rent of a shilling a year and subject to certain conditions: the front gardens had to remain as lawns which were mowed regularly on contract by the Trust; no flower borders or chains were allowed; and all the houses had to be painted the same colour. All that was welcomed by the owners and it set a standard for the years to come.

The owner of my house then was a master at Wellington College, Mr Gould, and a colleague of his, Mr Talboys, owned a cottage in The Croft. Both were bachelors, colourful personalities and strong-minded gentlemen. One result of this was that they frequently disagreed. It was during one of the periods when they were not on speaking terms that Mr Gould told me that he had had enough and that he would move away. That gave me an opening to ask if I might buy his house and, to my delight, he agreed. So the house became my property in 1947.

Mr Talboys and Mr Gould were outstanding intellectuals and as such were typical of a few other residents round about. This is brought out in what a former neighbour of mine wrote about my book *Within Living Memory: Recollections of Old Headington*. He said,

> I think the singular quality of Old Headington lies in so many cottagers being dons though living alongside normal human beings. Should not Don Salvador de Madariaga feature in the next edition, along with Mr Rollo St Clair

Talboys, the aesthete, who lived in The Croft, discovered the novelist Firbank, wrote the history of Wellington College, and made apt but discouraging remarks about everybody's furniture and sherry?

This little cameo refers to only a few of the people I knew at the time. If I were to widen the list with the shop-keepers, the 'cottagers', the professionals and the academics, the variety of those living in the village would certainly be underlined. Some folk needed knowing and understanding but all were interesting and a pleasure to have as friends.

Another drawing point is the somewhat unique geographical situation. The village is pleasantly hidden away in an oasis on the outskirts of Oxford. Its high walls and the variety of houses mostly built of that warm, friendly stone taken years ago from neighbouring quarries, grass verges and cobbled footways, are features which give it character. Those who have lived here have taken pride in their village and have done what they could to preserve it. Today the village is not only conveniently placed for the shops, transport and hospitals, but it is open to the surrounding countryside. So it is no wonder that it appeals to those whose work is with the several hospitals as well as to other professional people and rising business executives.

Situated as it is on a high shoulder of land several hundred feet above sea-level and higher than Oxford City, overlooking the junction of the Cherwell and the Thames, the climate is less enervating than that down in the valley. Hence the old saying

> Down in Oxford the air's like stale flat beer; up in Headington it's pure champagne.

Earlier sections of this book have dealt with the growth of Headington from earlier times so I will now confine myself to the twentieth century.

At the end of the nineteenth century there were no traffic problems. After a hundred years of a new road built by arrangement with the Turnpike Trust to bypass the old London road over Shotover, traffic was amounting to only a few thousand vehicles a week. Where the traffic lights are now was known as High Bush Cross. There was a small tollgate and turnpike house and it cost about a penny for a wagon and horse to pass through. To the south an avenue of chestnut trees led down Windmill Lane into open fields. The windmill, described in 1847 as

> lofty, powerful and substantial

High Bush Cross, about 1903

had long since disappeared (see drawing on p.55).

As the years passed, transport developed. There was the fly business of Papa Wells and Mr Dring's bus (The Rocket) to meet trains at the station, the horse trams, the early motor buses, etc., until today we have a regular service of local buses, coaches to London and the X70 coach to Heathrow and Gatwick.

Old Headington became bordered by the new London Road to the south, Old High Street in the west and the Bayswater valley to the north. On the other side of the London Road there is still the old stone-walled village of Quarry with its famous Morris dancers and, no doubt as of old,

The far end of Windmill Road near Rock Edge and the supposed site of the windmill

Bury Knowle House, much as in the 1930s; now an elegant Branch Library and clinic

pretty girls whose ancestors came from the tin mines of Cornwall where they seemed to have unusual irises in their beautiful eyes,

as I was told thirty years ago. In Old Headington a mixed community had for long been emerging, of large houses and small cottages, of the rich and the not so rich. But there is one sideline which could be most enlightening. To look into the stories of several of the large houses is to discover how Old Headington grew. What could be even more interesting would be to know a little of those dwellings which are known to have existed but which have now disappeared. Take, for instance, the three cottages which were once in Dunstan Road where the garden of West Lodge now is. We are told that Mrs Coppock, Tom Gammon, Florrie Brown and Mrs Parker lived there. Also to the right of the lodge of Headington House in The Croft there were two more cottages, one occupied by Mr Cove, the coachman, and the other by Mr Wingfield, the dairyman. There were also some almshouses just about there but little is known about their occupants. In The Croft next to The Bell public house there were two thatched cottages which were destroyed by fire, and so on. Fire damage was the cause of many dwellings, many of them thatched, disappearing in earlier years. These caused gaps in the village map which were not always wisely filled (see p.37). Did these little-known cottagers and their ancestors help to colour the history of the village? Over the years local industries had produced quarriers, stone-masons, tilemakers, thatchers, farriers, market gardeners and carriers, to say nothing of butchers and bakers. They all lived nearby.

Old Headington was taken over by the Oxford City Council in 1929, and in 1930 the Council also bought the Bury Knowle estate including the baby health clinic first begun in 1915. In 1932 Bury Knowle Park was opened to the public and the Branch Library followed. These amenities, together with improvements in drainage and street lighting, certainly enhanced the area.

The Second World War was to bring more changes. The younger men were leaving for the Forces and men and women at home were enrolling for Air Raid Precaution duties. Those I knew most about were my good friends and neighbours in Church Street. One was an eminent barrister, another a professional gardener in great demand, then there was a judge's daughter full of good works, and also a spinster who owned three or four magnificent white goats which she kept in the Laurel Farm garden. These people were just a few of the Air Raid Wardens on duty at odd times night and day. Their parading round the roads offered a chance to exercise the goats which

Mather's Farm, the original house of the Berry family

The local talking point

followed their owner almost to heel. That was a sight not to be forgotten. Some A.R.P. volunteers had duties further afield. My wife worked in the Control Room in the Town Hall, quite often on night duty, and she cycled there and back.

Oxford has always been known for its number of cyclists and there were even more of them during the war. Thomas Sharp in his *Oxford Replanned* (1948) wrote of them as coming

> in hordes, like locusts, upon the university town.

Recently we have heard ministerial admonition 'to get on your bikes' to go places both metaphorically and literally. Old Headington did not need to be told that. A friend of mine over many years is still more often seen with her bike than without it. She uses it constantly to go to the shops and so do other people use theirs. If anything, the habit is gaining ground. A recent census reported that some 26,000 cyclists commute to Oxford daily from the surrounding area. And the probability of so-called 'science parks' in Oxford could bring more.

After the war there were still some useful village stores. The corner shop and the Post Office opposite the Black Boy had been a general meeting place - call it a talking point if you like - passing through several hands since the 1870s. Soon after the war Mr and Mrs Bond took over. Literally their shop was in the heart of the village and the Bonds were dear to us all. Then there was Berry the Baker's and Berry the Butcher's (one cannot imagine the village without the Berry family) and the family name has until recently been on the window of the new delicatessen which is much appreciated. Sadly on 31 May 1987 the bakery closed after nearly a hundred years as the village shop. The delicatessen now trades under the name of 'Nina's'. Headington Produce opened about 1950 in the corner of North Place first for greengrocery and later for general grocery. It was unlikely that you would walk in the village or go into any of these shops without receiving a friendly word from people you knew and probably talking to the clergy of the parish. And many's the time I have taken one of my sons to watch Mr Stow at work in his forge.

It was a sociable, pleasant environment and it helped to build up morale after the dark war years. Something else was emerging too and that was an awareness of community life.

The Parish Church, the new Baptist Church and the Priory all arranged many social functions. St Andrew's Church, however, was looking to bigger things. Their idea was to organize a fête with entertainment for all the neighbourhood. The idea caught on and a large fête was held on 14 July 1953 on the Headington United Football Ground in Manor Road. More and bigger fêtes followed annually at Headington Church of England School, London Road, until 1958. Looking at the programme for that year I see that there was a Baby Show, a Models Exhibition, Races, Sea Scout Display, Miniature Railway, Side Shows, a professional Fashion Show and the City of Oxford Silver Band. That last fête which occupied many people for several weeks made over £400 - a good figure in 1958 - and it helped to swell the funds for the new Parish Hall.

In 1915 the Women's Institute movement was introduced to England from Canada. It quickly gained official support and Katharine Woods who had come to live in what is now Osler Road was urged to get a Branch started in Headington. This happened in 1918 with Mrs Olive Jacks of Shotover as its first President. Meetings were held at the British Workman but later the Headington Women's Institute moved to Highfield. Some forty-five years passed before Old Headington Women's Institute was formed with Mrs Cameron (Elizabeth Bowen, the novelist, who lived at White Lodge) as first President.

In May 1956 the community spirit showed itself again when an appeal for a new Parish Hall was launched. Hitherto there had been only a dilapidated small shed to serve as the Church parish room, Scout HQ, Committee room and general meeting place. This lack of accommodation was a great obstacle to the growth of the family life of St Andrew's. Northway Estate had been added to the parish and so far had no community centre. The need had been voiced by George Day, the previous Vicar, but now the new Vicar, Derek Eastman, supported by four Trustees, took responsibility for it and got things moving. Parties and sales of work were arranged and the collection of milk bottle tops organized among many other activities to raise cash for a new building to serve the church and the community. It was a tremendous effort by many people and the result was that by October 1958 the new hall became a reality. Headington Village Hall has been in regular use ever since and today it is difficult to get a booking in it.

Next we come to a development which goes to the heart of good neighbourliness. In 1961 after much thought and discussion locally, the Vicar and the local GP, becoming increasingly aware of situations where help was needed which could not be provided by existing organizations, planned a scheme to make those needs known to people likely to help. This was done under the name of the FISH Good Neighbour Scheme. (Fish had been a word widely used by the early Church and was based on the Greek word for fish, *Ichthus,* which consists of the initial letters of the words Jesus Christ, Son of God, Saviour). This scheme got off the ground quickly with an able adminstration. FISH became well known and soon the movement had spread not only throughout the United Kingdom but also to the United States of America and Canada. It still goes strong. Old Headington was its home and today membership is ecumenical and open to all. It can be said that the FISH scheme during its existence has done much to influence welfare work generally.

Fun and games in 1955

The lane outside Emden House, still much as it was

Open country at the rear of William Orchard Close

Such movements as I have just been describing gave the locality liveliness. That, together with the fact that it was a pleasant place in which to live, led to residents taking much interest in maintaining its village character. This has never meant that nothing new should be built nor old buildings restored, so much as that what was added should fit harmoniously between the present stone walls, buildings and open spaces. (For details of the Buchanan Study see p.52) The City Council always had been sympathetic to local feeling. Thus when the Parish Hall was opened the Council agreed to build a stone boundary wall round it in exchange for some land between it and the road. This made the turn into Dunstan road wider and safer.

It was in the year after this happened that a field north of the church was threatened by developers with a number of new houses which could mean new access roads, the demolition of a cottage of distinction and possible extension of the site later (see also p.49). To combat this threat and to guard against further encroachment into the green belt, the 'Friends of Old Headington' was formed to speak for the village to the City Council. The Council suggested some restriction to the plan, the developers appealed to the appropriate Ministry and the Friends tried to raise funds to support the Council's defence of its policy. The end of the conflict came in 1965 with the Ministry of Housing and Local Government upholding the Council's decision. The site was then offered for sale and bought by the Friends with money lent by individual residents to a non-profit making Trust. Five houses were built in the new William Orchard Close (see pp. 29 and 49) and in due course the loans were repaid. After this the Friends were recognized by the Council as a responsible body to whom planning applications might be shown for

The charm of The Croft, something which is unique and well worth preserving

comment. This link was strengthened when Old Headington became an official Conservation Area in 1971. Bury Knowle has recently been added to the Conservation Area.

Another long period of discussions between the Council and Old Headington started in 1975 when the Council bought the Laurel Farm site for housing (see also p.51). This new estate has now been completed and Laurel Farm Close has many attractive features. Certainly the Planning Committee of the City Council has given sensitive treatment to this development with the result that it fits well into the environment.

The Friends are much concerned about the density of traffic and parking in the area which has been steadily growing worse over recent years. On weekdays additional car parking is needed for shoppers and the staffs of shops and businesses, but on Oxford United match days the near-by roads are chock-a-block. No-one begrudges the club its successes, and it has many supporters in Headington, but it becomes ever more obvious that this First Division Club needs a new ground with space for large crowds and car parking outside the urban sprawl. Let us hope this chance will come sooner than we think!

Local groups of residents are in regular touch with the Police and the City Council who expect to issue shortly some suggestions for easing traffic problems. This is the position as I write. The hope is that as time passes some alleviation of this local nightmare will be possible.

The Friends of Old Headington is now a member society of the Oxford Preservation Trust who in recent years have given three awards for restoration work and new building in the Conservation Area.

The Croft has always been an area of special interest in the village and its character depends on the retention of the few small green spaces. The old Baptist church has been renovated imaginatively, but its charm will suffer if it is hemmed in with unsuitable infilling. This delightful and historic enclave deserves the careful attention it is receiving from both the Friends and the planning authorities. Together it is hoped to safeguard its future.

In 1986 the City Council's refusal to give planning permission for a two-storey house in The Croft was upheld by the Secretary of State for the Department of the Environment. Part of the Inspector's report has already been quoted on p.53, but his report also stated, on the question of access for cars,

> The Council are right to resist firmly the introduction of a development which would be likely to increase existing problems, even if only slightly.

This support was most encouraging.

In a lighter vein, each summer over recent years the Friends have organized an Open Gardens Sunday. A number of householders agree to open their gardens and the village is in festive mood for the afternoon, with teas available at the Village Hall. It usually draws a good crowd. This all adds to the friendly nature of the place, and visitors from a distance are not backward in speaking of its charm.

As I said when I began, by recalling some past happenings I hope that we have seen how the village has become a vibrant and mixed community of young and old from all walks of life. Certainly its members are individualistic and diverse, yet they are generally united in their love for the place where they live and they are concerned for its preservation. If some of that picture has come across in what I have written then this final section of the book will have achieved something of what it set out to do.

LESLIE TAYLOR *ex-publisher, is a member of the Oxford Preservation Trust and a Vice-President of the Friends of Old Headington.*

Bibliography

Arkell, W.J., *Oxford Stone* (London, 1947).

Buchanan, C. and Partners, *Old Headington Study* (1976).

Cam, H., 'The Hundred outside the North Gate of Oxford', in *Oxoniensia* vol.1 (1936).

Coppock, G.A. and Hill, B.M., *Headington Quarry and Shotover, a history* (Oxford, 1933).

Evans, E., 'The Manor Headington' in *Report of the Oxfordshire Archeological Society for 1928*.

Graham, M., *On foot in Oxford. No.5, Headington* (Oxfordshire County Libraries, 1986).

Headington Enclosure Map 1804, Oxfordshire County Record Office ref. Vol. F.

Hearne, T., *Remarks and Collections* vol.6 (1717-1719) ed. C.E. Doble (Oxfordshire Historical Society, 1902).

Hearth Tax Returns Oxfordshire 1665 ed. M.M.B. Weinstock (Oxfordshire Record Society, vol.21, 1940).

Jackson's Oxford Journal for 29 August 1835.

Jewitt, Ll., 'On Roman remains recently discovered at Headington', in *Journal of the British Archaeological Association* vol.5 (1850) and vol.6 (1851).

Kelly's Directories from 1817, and others, for Oxford and Oxfordshire.

Ordance Survey Map, 1st edition 1876. 1:2500

Oxford City Council, *Local Plan for Oxford* (Oxford, 1986).

Oxford City Council, *Old Headington Conservation Area* (Oxford, 1973).

Oxford Preservation Trust, *Twelfth Annual Report* (Oxford, 1939).

Oxfordshire County Council, *Structure Plan for Oxfordshire* (Oxford, 1979).

Oxfordshire County Council, *Structure Plan Review: Consultative Document* (Oxford, 1982).

Parker, J.H., 'On the wall paintings recently discovered in Headington church', in *Proceedings of the Oxford Architectural and Historical Society* n.s.vol.1 (1863).

Samuel, R., 'Quarry Roughs': life and labour in Headington Quarry, 1860-1920', in *Village Life and Labour*, ed. by R. Samuel (History workshop series, 1975).

Scargill, I. and Crosby, A., *Oxford and its Countryside* (Oxford, 1982).

Sharp, T., *Oxford Replanned* (Oxford, 1948).

Stenton, F.M., 'St. Frideswide and her Times', in *Oxoniensia* vol.1 (1936).

Taylor, L. and G., *Within Living Memory: Recollections of Old Headington* (Headington, 1978).

Victoria County History: Oxfordshire, vol.5, 'Bullingdon Hundred', ed. M. Lobel (1957).

Young, C.J., *The Roman Pottery Industry of the Oxford Region* (Oxford, British Archaeologial reports, 1977).